If you're hurting, you need to read this book! If you know someone who's hurting, read this book and give it to your friend who's hurting! If you've been let down, hurt, or even betrayed by someone you've trusted, you must read this book! If you feel that God has somehow not been the God you expected or trusted, you need this book! Jay is a powerful speaker who has a simple, easy-to-understand way of helping anyone get through the kinds of struggles we all face at times. He's a storyteller—and a very good one. His stories—about friends, strangers, and even himself—are riveting! I dare you to try to lay this book down in the middle of reading one of them!

—JIMMY HOUSTON
HOST, *JIMMY HOUSTON OUTDOORS*

Jay Lowder has a gift, an ability to pull you into the very scene of the stories and encounters in his book. Some call it "a way with words." I call it a gift. Jay helps reveal to us all the opportunity to reflect on our own experiences in life. The only difference is his sincere, honest, and open approach to finding a solution or resolution through love and forgiveness.

—LUKE MCCOWN
NFL QUARTERBACK

Love and goodness come to life in the stories he shares in this book. This man inspires me—and I know his book will do the same for you.

—J. LEE GRADY
AUTHOR, DIRECTOR OF ⌐

D1059425

If "writing what you know" is the key to an author's success, then Jay Lowder is well on his way. Jay does not presume to instruct readers on "how to" overcome life's hurdles, as it's clear he himself is still a work in progress. But through the power of story his anecdotal insights provide a portal into his life, mind, and heart—warts and all. If the man on the platform can be so transparent as to admit he too questions his own spirituality, faith, love, hope, and failure, how can we not be similarly challenged to the same admission and driven to seek answers from the same source? Jay is not trying to pull us up the mountain where he has attained perfection. Instead, he is trying to direct us and drive each of us to find and fuel our own way.

—Larry Ross
President, A. Larry Ross Communications
Director of Media Relations for Billy Graham

MIDNIGHT IN AISLE

7

JAY LOWDER

PASSIO

Most CHARISMA HOUSE BOOK GROUP products are available at special quantity discounts for bulk purchase for sales promotions, premiums, fund-raising, and educational needs. For details, write Charisma House Book Group, 600 Rinehart Road, Lake Mary, Florida 32746, or telephone (407) 333-0600.

MIDNIGHT IN AISLE SEVEN by Jay Lowder
Published by Passio
Charisma Media/Charisma House Book Group
600 Rinehart Road
Lake Mary, Florida 32746
www.charismahouse.com

Cover design by Kent Jensen / Knail, LLC
Design Director: Bill Johnson

Visit the author's website at www.jaylowder.com.

Library of Congress Control Number: 2012940049
International Standard Book Number: 978-1-61638-608-5
E-book ISBN: 978-1-61638-867-6

Some names, places, and identifying details with regard to stories in this book have been changed to help protect the privacy of the individuals involved.

First edition

12 13 14 15 16 — 987654321
Printed in the United States of America

DEDICATION

To my gorgeous wife, Missy—if I had a million lives, I would spend them all with you. You have made so many sacrifices to enable me to chase my dreams.

Mom and Dad—what little good has come from my life is because of your influence and the foundation you laid for me.

Hollis and Donna—if any couple is leaving behind a legacy, you are. Your friendship is an incredible gift.

I love you and appreciate you all. Without each of you I would amount to much less.

CONTENTS

FOREWORD

I MET JAY LOWDER about seven years ago at an event in Texas where I was scheduled to sing and he was to speak. As a musician I have shared the platform with dozens of speakers, but I will never forget the day I met Jay. From the moment we started talking, I knew there was something different about this guy and that a lifelong friendship was beginning. The moment felt surreal, as if we were destined to meet.

Jay grew up in a well-to-do family, but he understands struggles. He's had his fair share, much like the ones you or I have experienced. As Jay and I talked, he never put on airs but was real, straightforward, and transparent. Perhaps the most important thing I heard the day we first met was the love in his voice. He has a big heart and great passion for people.

Anyone can be a good public speaker if he practices long enough, but there are some things that even the best speakers cannot be taught. It is that ability to do more than give an inspiring talk but to actually touch someone's heart. I have been on stage with numerous people, and I haven't seen many who can influence people the way Jay can. It is an even bigger blessing to see him in his day-to-day interaction with people, because he isn't any different on stage than he is off.

Jay has the uncanny ability to meet people where they are, no matter where that place is. Whether he is talking with the rich or poor, a waitress, or a bank president, he can find a story to bring hope and encouragement to their level.

Through the stories in this book, including Jay's personal story of nearly taking his own life, I believe you will see that life is not a series of random events. We are being led by something much greater than ourselves. In this book Jay shows how our pain, hurt, and shame can be covered with grace, hope, and forgiveness.

As I read these real-life stories, I was on the edge of my seat, anxious to know what would happen next. I couldn't put the book down. It left me wanting more—to love more, serve more, and be a better example to others. I know after you read this you will understand exactly what I mean. This book will challenge and inspire you to examine your own actions and look for opportunities to reach out to the world around you.

—Jason Crabb
Grammy- and Dove Award–Winning Recording Artist

INTRODUCTION

I AM FASCINATED BY a compelling true story. When I was a young boy, I loved to hear my grandfather tell stories about his days as a soldier and his travels around the world. They captivated my imagination and prompted me to secretly dream of living an adventurous, meaningful, heroic life. His stories also taught me that one of the best ways to avoid making painful, wrong decisions is to learn from the successes and failures of others. This book is a reflection of that conviction.

As an intense twenty-one-year-old man, I found myself losing life's tug of war. With the little rope I had left slipping from my weary grasp, I decided to give up my quest for purpose and end the pain. I pointed a revolver to my temple and prepared to close the final door. Isolated and alone, I became convinced no one understood my despair. Most don't take the drastic measures I contemplated, but in time I realized there were scores of people like me who were struggling to fill the vacancies and voids in what seemed like a pointless existence.

Life's greatest mysteries are often illuminated in the most unexpected places through the most unlikely encounters at the most unforeseen times. Three weeks ago I was reminded of this truth while spending the better part of my evening visiting with men living on death row. The last thing I expected was to hear the stories of faith and hope shared within those prison walls.

Unforgettable experiences and people have helped bring this book into being. Within these pages are the stories of how one lost man and others like me found identity, forgiveness, direction, faith, and significance. I do not offer you a miracle manual, step-by-step process, or quick fix. To me, sugarcoated solutions have very little impact. What I do present are the raw, hopeful, genuine, messy accounts of real people, including myself, in hopes that they can serve as a type of compass in your search for meaning. The greatest task for any person is to discover purpose in his or her life.

There are many ways to communicate information, but I have found that some truths are most easily grasped in the context of a parable. By definition, a parable is a simple story meant to illustrate a moral, intellectual, emotional, social, or spiritual lesson. The following parable stories are personal, real encounters that present lessons about life, love, God, and purpose but in an unusual format. Each chapter stands independent of the others and has its own central focus.

My inclusion of the stories in this book should not be seen as an endorsement of all the choices the individuals made. I merely present them and leave you to draw the conclusions. I make no claims to be an expert. I am only a man with numerous flaws and scars who has escaped to find freedom, satisfaction, and complete peace.

Of all the projects I've ever undertaken, none has been more difficult or rewarding as this. Countless hours have been invested with the goal of providing hope to multitudes of hurting people looking for answers to some of life's most difficult questions.

Undeniably and without apology my faith plays the biggest role in my outlook and viewpoints on life. Regrettably, I am not always a perfect example of what I say I believe. Maybe you have been betrayed by someone like me, who claimed an allegiance to Christ. Perhaps your greatest hurts came at the hands of the religious. Maybe you're convinced people who call themselves believers in Jesus are not compassionate or loving but just narrow-minded critics of anyone who does not embrace their opinions.

I don't fault you for drawing these conclusions. I was once one of those people who called themselves a Christian and was everything except a good example of Christ. Many of the accusations made against people of faith are deserved and earned. However, as you read the following pages, I hope you can objectively consider that the picture of God that has been painted for you may not be a true representation of who He really is. Perhaps you can find what many of the people in this book have found, which is a love, understanding, and hope they never thought possible.

Some of you have been followers of Jesus for years, but you feel abandoned and injured by Him. Instead of living the abundant life you dreamed of, you're limping along through a series of monotonous days. God seems a million miles away.

No matter how bleak reality seems, He has much more for you. I hope you can discover the beauty, healing, destiny, and wonder I have found through the lives I have written about. Their stories have given me assurance that I am not forsaken. I hope they also will help you discover, or rediscover, that neither are you.

Chapter 1

PRISON BREAK

I HAVE NEVER BEEN sentenced to prison or jail, but I have been locked up many times. My cell has been lonely, dark, isolating, and cold. I have met a lot of prisoners just like me. It gives me some comfort knowing I am not the only one. It is always easier to justify failure when you have a companion.

Some of my former cellmates could easily be detected as offenders, but many others are not so easy to identify. Some reveal their chains through sarcastic and bitter words; others do not have to speak. The lines and expressions on their faces tell what words dare not say, their countenance revealing the deepest and most private suffering.

People in prison respond to incarceration in different ways. Some accept their sentences, while others spend every waking moment trying to find a way of escape. I have visited numerous prisons and jails where I have been amazed to meet people who say they never want to leave. Prison has become the only way of life they know and the only place they have respect and friends. They say they have nothing on the outside to go back to and have become comfortable locked up.

I guess if you stay in any place long enough, even when it is the wrong one, it can begin to feel like home. Maybe this is why the number of people who leave prison only to return is sky high. Men have tendencies: the things we should not do come naturally, while the things we should do are so hard to get done. Just because you take the man out of the big house doesn't mean you've taken the big house out of the man.

On the other hand, the prisoner consumed with escaping does so because he is dying—not a literal death, but the death of his will and hope for a better life. It is the death that comes when your heart gives up any chance for change or to live a life of purpose. Everyone dies, but only a few truly live. These captives want more than the air they breathe; they want a life that truly has meaning.

There are many types of prisons. Some have literal bars and fences, while others use emotions, habits, and thoughts to hold its captives. So which prison held me? It is the prison of rejection. It can be found in the hearts of broken sons, discarded wives, lost teens, abused women, and neglected children as well as the successful, prominent, educated, and religious. People find themselves locked in the prison of rejection because they committed one of two crimes: either they were unwilling to accept others, or they were not accepted themselves. In my case it was...wait, let me first explain.

I was born and raised in north Texas and live there now. Although there are many places in the state that are beautiful, they are not here in the far northern part (no matter what the locals say). I have spent the lion's share of my life on the road. I have visited every state in the United States except four, and I have seen quite a bit of the Lone Star State. Yet I have never witnessed as many unusual sights as I have here.

One particular sight that has intrigued me for some time is a tiny jail in a town of less than one thousand people. It is said to be one of the oldest jails in Texas and is located on the highway between Wichita Falls and Lubbock, Texas. If you have ever seen the movie *Lonesome Dove* (considered a masterpiece here in Texas), then you can imagine this being the jail where Blue Duck was held before he jumped out the second-story window to his death. The jail is over one hundred years old and easily looks twice that.

Out front stands an old tree. After its leaves fall, the crusty, crooked branches resemble the hands of an evil witch reaching toward the walls. The jail has sleeping quarters that will house four men upstairs and the same number of women downstairs. It was even built with a trap door for "hanging" offenders. There is a famous story of three inmates who murdered the on-duty sheriff in an attempt to escape. The three were quickly reapprehended then swiftly tried and convicted.

I passed by this old jail every few months in my travels, and something about it always jerked at my curious mind. Although I felt a pull to stop and check it out, I was always too busy to break down and do so until one moonlit morning at about twelve thirty. Two friends were riding with me on our way back home from an event when we drove past the jail. We still had a couple hours more to drive, but when I looked out the window and saw the outline of the jail, I could not resist.

I made an illegal U-turn, parked out front, and walked through a door that was faintly ajar. A slightly startled woman sitting at an old wooden desk looked up quickly and asked if she could help. I began to explain my long-standing fascination with the old jail. I told her my friends and I were passing through, and I could no longer resist the urge to stop. This jailer was a welcoming woman who surprised me when she recognized my name.

"I thought you looked familiar. I know who you are. This weekend I heard a radio advertisement about the Outdoor Extravaganza you were speaking at and thought it would be something my youngest would enjoy doing. He loves hunting and fishing, and we spent yesterday at your event in Lubbock."

I thought it was highly unlikely that this was a coincidence, and I felt a chill sprint up my spine. It seemed too perfect after passing by all these times that I would just happen to stop the day after this woman heard my name on the radio. She cordially invited my friends and me to glance around the jail as she explained its history. Because there were no women locked up, she let us see the female quarters located on the bottom floor.

After about ten minutes of small talk and gander we were about to leave. When I asked how many men were upstairs, a strange expression washed over the jailer's face. Then she asked, "Would you like to go up and speak to the inmates? They have very few visitors, and even though it is late, I think they would be glad to see a new face and hear what you have to say."

I told her I would be glad to talk with them so long as I did not interrupt their sleep. As soon as I got the words out of my mouth, she grabbed her antique-looking keys and motioned for all three of us to follow her.

Upon climbing the old staircase, we were immediately met by a curious group of four wide-awake men. I introduced myself and my comrades, shook their hands, and began to explain how we ended up visiting the jail. All four of the men crowded near the bars and listened intently to every word I spoke.

First impressions last forever. Two of the men stood out to me instantly. One was a gregarious Hispanic guy with a big personality, and the other was a young, quiet guy who looked like he still belonged in high school. I tried to offer encouragement by telling them we all make mistakes we can learn from. I discussed how the crime that landed them in trouble could be the catalyst that transforms their lives for the better if they are willing to own it and learn from it. Reactions to events can sometimes be more important than actions in events.

I talked about letting go of the past because it can't be changed and seizing whatever opportunities were before them. I did not offer some hokey religious platitude about letting go and letting God. I just tried to be transparent and show the concern I genuinely felt. I also listened to them. If you tune in to someone's words for very long, those words will reveal what is hidden in that person's heart.

The youngest inmate vented about how he was twenty-one and in two days was being transferred to a prison in Huntsville, Texas, where he would begin a twenty-five-year sentence without the possibility of parole. He said his father would not visit him, and all his mother could do was cry the two times she came to see him. I didn't know what crime he committed, but my heart went out to him. When it was time to go, I asked the men if I could pray for them. It was the best thing I had to offer. They were all in favor. Nothing makes people more open to prayer than getting in a bind they cannot get out of on their own.

Afterward I began shaking their hands through the steel bars and wishing the guys my best. I also offered my address in case they wanted to write. The last one in line was the young, baby-faced guy who on his way to the pen. I obviously did not know him, but I felt a deep sense of compassion toward him. The whole time I was with the inmates, I was troubled that someone so young was losing so much of his life.

Before I left, I expressed exactly what I felt boiling inside me. "Hey, man. I do not know what you have done to get twenty-five years, and I do not care. It is never too late to change and to start anew. Your life is not over. Prison can be a time of getting your education, working through your issues, and learning how you can help others. Do not give up, bro. I do not judge you, but I love you man." I meant every word...or so I thought.

Walking downstairs, I felt sickened to see such a young life being crushed. My mind kept tripping over what this boy could have done wrong. After explaining my gratitude to the jailer, I told my companions to wait for me in the car. I then broke a cardinal rule that I established when visiting correctional facilities. I never, ever ask what crime someone has committed because I do not want my opinion to be skewed by the revelation of someone's past. But with this guy I just could not resist.

"Ma'am, I have never asked this question about any inmate before, but I have to know, what crime has the boy committed?" I explained that I felt some kind of connection to him and wanted to help.

She replied, "Are you sure you want to know?"

When I said, "Yes, I am sure," I knew the answer was destined to haunt me. I had no idea how much.

The jailer's words left me feeling nauseated. I acted like I was unfazed, but I could feel my heart racing. After telling the jailer good-bye, I walked out to my car, wanting to hit something to unleash the anger I felt. Drunk with fury, I turned into a Jekyll and Hyde. If you have ever seen one of those "when animals go bad" videos, then you can imagine my transformation. For the next two hours of driving I tried to overcome the rage I felt. I knew it was wrong, but I couldn't seem to shake it. After getting home, I lay in bed until 5:30 a.m. completely unable to sleep.

Two days later I was not only struggling with the fact that this man had committed such a horrible crime but also with how I could so easily turn on someone I genuinely thought I cared for. As far as I knew, I did not hate anyone and could not remember anyone in my past I had not forgiven or was holding a grudge against. Why did I feel such hatred toward this man?

The old saying is true: hating and refusing to forgive someone is like drinking poison and expecting the other person to die. I knew I had to do something. I decided to call my best friend for advice on how to shake the problem because nothing seemed to help. In the days I spent wrestling with my anger toward the man, I began to revisit the circumstances surrounding the only other person I could remember hating: my oldest sister.

My sister is quite beautiful and intelligent. She was also quite rebellious and stubborn in her high school days. It was not uncommon for her and our parents to be at odds. Sometimes the conflict erupted in a volcano of anger and hurt that spewed everywhere. My sister and I were fairly close when we were young, but in time the distance grew beyond measure. The wall between us seemed to sprout up suddenly, like a new building that just appears before you even knew it was being built.

In my own self-centered world of girls, cars, and parties, I was oblivious to the struggles she was facing. One weekend during my senior year of high school, her friend called when our parents were out of town to give me some unexpected news. "Jay, I think you need to know your sister, Kay, is gay." I immediately jumped in the car and drove to Kay's apartment to confront her. I had to make sure it was a lie.

When no one came to the door, I left a message on her voice mail and waited in her parking lot until 3:00 a.m., but she never came home. The next day I continued my stakeout and knew something was wrong when she kept avoiding me. Late one afternoon I saw her car on the road and raced up beside her, rolled down the window, and yelled, "Pull over; we've got to talk."

She knew why I was chasing her, because the girl who called me also phoned her to give her fair warning. Kay yelled back from her car, "We have nothing to talk about," and tried to speed away. She pulled over only when I threatened to run her off the road.

I confronted her with what I had been told, and she admitted that it all was true. I incorrectly reacted in anger and disbelief, unleashing on her every disgusting ounce of my judgment and rejection. After many jagged words were spoken, the conversation ended with her telling me it was her life and I should want her to be happy and me responding, "I hate you." I was convinced I had every right to reject her. That misplaced confidence only grew after an incident a few months later really sent me over the edge.

It happened at lunch late in my senior year. Because my school was close to the house, I often drove home for my thirty-minute lunch break just to see the family. At the time everything was going along great, and my sister and I had turned a new corner. A few weeks earlier, Kay had moved back home and told my parents she wanted out of her lifestyle. We had a tearful reunion and were putting the pieces back together.

But upon arriving home for lunch, I found my mom and dad sitting at the kitchen table, and Dad was doing something I couldn't remember seeing him do before. Dad was crying. He had tears running down his face, and Mom's eyes were also swollen, as if she had been punched. As far as I remembered, Dad did not even cry when his father died. Seeing him upset was a stab in the heart I could not take.

"What is going on?" I thundered. My parents replied that my sister was moving back in with her girlfriend. I rushed into my sister's room and started cursing, telling her that she was tearing the family apart by leaving. Kay just continued packing, as if unfazed by how much Mom and Dad were hurting. That took my anger to a boiling point. Kay yelled that her life was none of my business and I needed to stay out of it. I begged her to stay, for Mom and Dad's sake, but she said nothing could stop her from leaving. That's when I exploded.

I'd never pushed around a girl before and haven't since, but that day I pinned my sister against the wall and spewed my venom. The confrontation ended with me telling her I never wanted to see her again. I knew as I walked past Mom and Dad and out the door that my actions had hurt them as well, but I didn't care. I thought I had every right to shove my sister—out of my way and out of my mind.

As the months rolled by, I did not ask my parents about Kay and tried to ignore the situation all together. I believed the ridiculous notion that if I avoided something long enough, the issue would either work itself out or disappear. I was still too young to understand acceptance, forgiveness, and love are not meant to be earned but to be given freely. I also could not wrap my mind around the fact that forgiveness is denied to those who are unwilling to dispense it. Therefore I just moved on, or so I thought.

For the next three years I viewed Kay as an embarrassment to our family and me. There were times when she would come home for a few weeks, which my parents and I always took to mean she was abandoning her lifestyle. But then she'd move out again, and each time it felt like she was turning her back on the family all over again. The emotional roller coaster we were all on kept the tension in the family thick. Mom and Dad became reluctantly accustomed to her chair being empty at Thanksgiving and Christmas, but it was fine with me.

When Kay hurt Mom and Dad, I took it as a personal assault. No doubt many of my own actions had hurt them as deeply as my sister's, but that was easy for me to dismiss. Although my anger wasn't justified, I thought it was. I had a legalistic, self-righteous view that I learned in part from some of the religious folks at church. Tragically, false religion taught me how to push away people who were different rather than to love and seek to understand them.

My anger was also due to pride. Rather than being concerned about my relationship with Kay, I became focused on what my narrow circle of friends might think of our family and me. Their opinions should never have been my priority, but I thought rejecting my sister would build walls protecting me from their condemnation. In actuality I was closing myself off from one of the people who should have meant the most to me, and I was becoming hard, skeptical, and angry. The criticism and isolation I was dishing out was doing nothing to alter Kay, but it was definitely changing me.

I had no idea at the time that I was bound in a prison of my own making. I had no idea that I was not living the fulfilling life I longed for because I refused to deal with the anger and unforgiveness that was destroying me.

When I hit twenty-one, I experienced a watershed event that began to change my perspective. I began to see how far I was from becoming the man I'd hoped to be. It did not happen all at once, but the scales began to fall, and I found myself wanting to repair the dam in my relationship with Kay. So I called her in Dallas and asked if we could meet. I knew she was a hundred and twenty miles away, but I had no idea how far that two-hour drive would actually take me.

Upon arriving at Kay's house, I admitted my faults and asked for forgiveness. I didn't expect anything in return. I was just worried that she would not believe my words because I hadn't done anything to prove my sincerity. I had hurt her tremendously both in word and deed, wrongly thinking I had a right to reject her because of the life she was living. It was an amazing moment for me when, after two hours of talking about all the mistakes we both had made, Kay and I hugged. I told her I loved her and that I was glad she was my sister. She replied, "I love you too, brother, and I forgive you. I really do." The road to a real relationship was not completely paved that night, but it was under good construction.

It has been years now, and I can honestly say my sister and I are closer than ever. She does not have to do any-thing to earn my love. I drove home from Dallas realizing that while I thought I was letting her out of a cage, I was actually the one who needed to be set free.

That night at the old jail when I asked the jailer what crime the young man had committed, she had motioned for me to sit in a chair before she answered.

"Jay, he is going to Huntsville because he raped two pre-teen girls."

I swallowed hard, partly because the girls he assaulted were the age of my only daughter. She offered a few more details before I walked out the door.

As I walked to the car, I thought about a male nurse

who once sat next to me at an event where I was scheduled to speak. He asked if I had heard the news about the two-year-old girl who was expected to die after being raped by her drug-crazed stepdad. He was the nurse on duty when she was brought in, and he was still pretty shaken up. I was supposed to be talking to a crowd of church people in a matter of moments and found myself silently calling the offender the worst names possible. I felt like such a hypocrite, but the emotions were hard to lasso.

I have seen the effects of sexual abuse in my most coveted relationship, which is with my wife. A family member sexually assaulted her for years, and it wreaked havoc not only on her personally but also on our marriage. If there was anything that got under my skin, it was sexual crimes. The inmate had struck a tender nerve. I believed he had not only tried to crucify and steal the innocent girls' present but their future as well. I was livid, because I know the cuts of sexual abuse are the hardest to heal. The scabs keep tearing off, leaving victims with a sense of guilt and unworthiness due to something that was no fault of their own.

Three sleepless nights after leaving the jail, I got a revelation about accepting others. I had vengeful thoughts about the boy I'd met. I am not proud to own them, but I secretly hoped he would burn in hell. I told my best friend that justice would seek and find him behind the walls of the Huntsville prison. I concluded that if anyone was beyond forgiveness and restoration, he was. I surmised that I might be responsible to forgive and accept some people but not everyone. I was convinced I was judge and jury when it came to who deserved my pardon and who did not. I was so wrong.

What about my own guilt? I have never been unfaithful to my wife, but I have entertained lustful thoughts. I have not been involved in a murder, but what about that hatred I have harbored? I have not been involved in a same-sex relationship, but what about my promiscuity before I was married? My failures are no less sinful than anyone else's.

Judging others only produces self-judgment. I was taught early on to love the sinner and hate the sin, but often that is just religious jargon, a masquerade to hide our judgmental attitudes. Who am I to despise anyone else's faults when I should be busy enough hating my own? Instead of shifting blame away from my own shortcomings, I should be reaching out to those who may not know that God is not the one condemning them. Tragically, many people are isolating the very people who need them the most.

Jesus never favored the religious; His darlings were always the hurting and the sinful, not the self-righteous. He never tired of showing His love for renegades. It is ironic that we tend to be drawn the least to the people He was drawn to the most. Jesus was regularly seen eating and spending time with outcasts and those we wickedly condemn. Unlike us He had an uncanny ability to make the losers of the world feel like the winners. He not only made them feel like somebody, but He also helped them to become somebody. We see people for who they were and are, but God sees people for who they have the potential to become.

Sadly, many morally superior people fall into the trap of loving only those who think, dress, act, and believe as they do. It is easy to beat your chest and say you are standing for truth without considering whose truth you are standing for. It's time for us to stop hating and start liberating. It's time to bury our legalistic and narcissistic actions. I do not claim to know everything about God, but I do know He loves and unconditionally accepts anyone who is willing to turn to Him. This includes thieves, robbers, murderers, drunks, adulterers, Muslims, homosexuals, gossipers, cheaters, fornicators, liars, hypocrites like me, and even those whom I have the hardest time loving: child abusers.

I asked God why He allowed me to stop at the old jail that night. Many people believe in coincidences, but I do not. I am sure every step I take has a purpose, a lesson, even beneficial pain if I am willing to embrace it. As I prayed for understanding, a question popped in my mind. Does God love the rapist in the Huntsville prison, and could even someone like him be forgiven?

As much as I wanted to deny it, I knew there was only one answer: yes. I believe God allowed me to meet that man so I could understand that He does not see others as I do. My love has boundaries, but His has no end. Although God does not accept all the things I do, He is willing to accept all of me. This is the love I still do not completely understand. Yet it is exactly the kind of love I want to give.

Chapter 2

BAREFOOT IN THE SNOW

THE COLD OF winter has a soothing effect on me. It's my favorite time of the year. There is nothing I enjoy more than building a fire on a frigid night, staring at hypnotic flames and iridescent embers, and smelling burning mesquite wood while drinking warm apple cider next to my yellow Lab and Great Pyrenees.

It can get extremely cold and windy in north Texas—during winter, locals say the only thing between here and the North Pole is a barbed wire fence, and it's usually down—yet my heart yearns for the northern winds. I love all the pleasures that come with this time of year—the shorter days, long nights, ruby red pomegranates, flannel sheets, hockey, Christmas and New Year's, all three of my children's birthdays, and, most of all, the falling of puffy white snowflakes.

Old Man Winter also slows down my speaking schedule, which means I can spend most of my time at home with my family instead of flying through the air on steel horses. Although I go to the office most days, it's not uncommon for me to hang out at home and unplug for a while. Sometimes it feels good to shrink the circle of conversation and get away from my routine. It can also get mundane.

Like some people I know who have retired, I became disillusioned with my time off a few winters ago. I began to feel nonproductive and in a rut. At the time I didn't have a large staff, only a part-time secretary. When I did go to the office, I was often alone, leaving me to feel somewhat isolated.

One frosty December morning while getting dressed for the day, I felt prompted to make a specific but off-the-cuff request to God. I said, "God, I am thankful for the spare time to spend with my wife and kids, but I still want to help others as well. If You know someone who is looking for You and place them in my path, I would be willing to tell them how to find You."

It was a simple but unlikely prayer. After all, my kids wouldn't be home until the afternoon, and nobody would be in the office that day. It had been weeks since I met anyone new. The freezing temperatures combined with the biting winds were keeping most folks behind closed doors.

Fifteen minutes later I had already forgotten the prayer as I pulled my truck up to the stop sign located less than fifty yards from my front door. As I looked to the right and left for oncoming traffic, I noticed a man right in front of me. He was on his knees, face to the ground, in a field owned by the Methodist church.

I leaned forward toward the windshield to get a better view, but my breath fogged the glass. As I wiped away the cloud, I began to wonder if the man was dead. His back was facing toward me, and the only thing moving were the tails from his untucked long-sleeve shirt. He wasn't wearing shoes or a coat.

Seconds later I saw him move slightly. When I realized he was alive, I began to wonder if he was insane. Nobody in his right mind would be out in this frigid weather without proper attire. And why was he on his knees in a vacant field? When people aren't sure what to do, they normally do nothing, which is exactly why I pulled over to the curb and sat motionless in my truck, frozen by the cold temperature and indecision.

Then I saw it. I don't know how I possibly could have missed it. After all, I have lived in the same house for years, and I have driven past this field thousands of times. This man wasn't just on his knees in a field. He was kneeling at the foot of a huge iron cross the church had erected many years before. It was originally painted white, but over time the paint had chipped off and the elements had turned it a rusty orange. It was dilapidated and ugly, almost to the point of being offensive.

Some things don't change in two millennia. Even though I knew it was there, I was too busy watching the man to notice the cross.

Stalling in my truck, I debated my next move. I needed to run some errands, and I thought briefly there was no sense getting out in the cold to deal with somebody who was crazy, demented, or both. But I couldn't resist. I put the truck and my reluctance in park, zipped my coat, and began walking toward the mysterious man.

Since I was coming from behind him, I felt it necessary to try not to startle him. Because of the howling wind I had to raise my voice as I approached from a distance. "Sir? Sir? Excuse me, sir!" There was no response, so I spoke a little louder. "Sir, are you OK?" He still wouldn't turn around, and I began to wonder if this man was waiting to attack me. I then looped around to his side to get a look at his face.

I was standing a few feet away, but the man kept his forehead to the ground. I squatted down to ground level and gently put my hand on his shoulder. "Can I help you, sir?" I was almost startled when he finally began to move. Slowly he leaned back, sat on his heels, and started wiping fresh tears with the palms of his hands. Neither of us spoke.

The young man, who appeared to be in his mid-twenties, continued to look down or away from me until finally he muttered softly, "My grandmother always told me, if you ever get into trouble, you go to the cross. Since this is the only cross I know of and since I'm in trouble, I came here." I knew his grandmother didn't mean for him to literally go to a cross, but I also knew desperate men will take desperate measures.

I instantly felt stirred, because I was in the presence of a person who was so in need of God he would do something so extreme. In a strange way I felt envious that his hunger for God in that moment was so much deeper than my own.

Then I remembered telling God if He sent someone my way who was looking for Him, I would tell that person how He could be found. Energized by the thought, I said, "My name is Jay. I don't know if you want to talk about what's going on, but I have to tell you what happened thirty minutes ago when I was getting ready. I'm pretty certain it had to do with meeting you." I briefly told him what I promised God and why.

It was obvious from his expression that he felt the same spiritual shock that was coursing through me. He held out his wet hand for me to shake then said, "I'm Grant. Thanks for caring enough to stop. I have so many problems. I have been out of work for months, I own an addiction I can't beat, and my marriage is falling apart. This morning I got into a war with my wife, and she kicked me out of the house.

"When she told me not to come back, I was so tore up that I walked out before grabbing my shoes or coat. I didn't know where to go or what to do, so I just drove around until I recalled what Grandma used to tell me as a boy. Her words kept running through my mind, 'Go to the cross. Go to the cross.' Then I remembered seeing this cross years ago, so I just came here. I didn't know what else to do."

Sometimes seeds of advice don't grow for years.

After hearing his story and his impossible timing, I knew God was determined we meet. What was the likelihood that he would just happen to stop at this cross minutes before I left my house? I began telling him how I got into my own pit of trouble years earlier and how I realized no one else could rescue me or fix my situation except Jesus. We had talked for several minutes when he asked me if I thought God could forgive someone as "screwed up" as he was.

After I assured him that God was willing to forgive him no matter what he'd gotten himself into, the man asked me how he could have Jesus in his life. I gave him a simple explanation, then he raised his eyebrows and said, "Could you help me to pray the kind of prayer you prayed when you accepted Him into your life?" Before I could say yes, he added, "Do you think we could do it right now?"

That's exactly what we did, and as soon as I said amen, he patted me on the back again and again, then hugged me like I had known him my entire life. His eyes were watering again, this time for a completely different reason. I felt honored to meet him, to watch this collision between heaven and earth, and he was clearly honored to meet God through a prayer of faith.

Cranked up from the experience, I explained that I lived across the street and would like him to come over to meet my wife. I also wanted to write down my cell number so we could stay in touch. Normally I would never expose my family to complete strangers, but Grant was different; plus, I was confident our meeting had been ordained.

When I bolted into the house, Grant waited on the porch. I couldn't contain my excitement as I hurried my dazed wife to change out of her pajamas so she could meet the man I found across the street. Minutes later Grant was standing in the kitchen, and we were both rattling off the story. Missy was blown away. She said in all her life she had never witnessed someone so touched by the hand of God. Before he left, we all hugged.

As I walked Grant to his car, I encouraged him to go home, apologize to his wife, tell her what had happened at the cross, and call me with a report. In the meantime

I would check my connections to try to find him a job. Later that night when Grant called, he sounded full of hope. He told me he rushed home only to find his wife, Chris, sound asleep on the couch. Rather than wake her up, he decided to write a note and place it on her chest before leaving to go look for day labor. The note simply read, "I'm sorry. Please forgive me. I received Jesus into my life today, and you have a brand-new husband."

He returned home a couple hours later, unsure what to expect. He wondered if Chris would believe him or just assume he was giving her another one of his lines to keep her from divorcing him. Chris met him at the door, curious, skeptical, and confused by the note. When he explained the full story of his revolution at the cross, she told him she was willing to work through their fractured marriage.

I was thrilled to hear his report and eager to share some news of my own. I knew Grant's life would never be the same, but I also knew he needed someone to help him get on his feet with a job. He had been knocked down by life; most of the punches could be attributed to some really bad decisions. But that was no excuse to neglect a need, especially when he had two children and Christmas was around the corner. I've always believed that hurting people need to be shown how much you care as much as, or more than, they need to be told.

I don't remember my dad saying this to me, but I do recall him demonstrating it countless times. He regularly picked up complete strangers, bought families groceries, paid people's rent—all without giving any of them a lecture or a condemning look. Whenever he saw a need, he didn't pray for someone else to come along and meet it. He met it himself. Dad never preached a sermon in church, but he never needed to. His life was a sermon. He reminds me of another Man who often touched people's stomachs before He attempted to touch their hearts. Maybe my father's example explains why I was so intent on helping Grant find work.

When Grant finally finished updating me on what happened between him and Chris, I told him I was able to find him a seasonal job through a friend. I also asked if he, Chris, and their children would join us for dinner the following day. While we ate together, I asked Chris what she thought when she found Grant's note. It is one thing for a man to say he has changed, but his wife knows if he's genuine. She softly said, "I thought it was another scheme until I saw his face."

I asked her to explain, and she had trouble putting it into words. "It doesn't make sense. I know him better than anyone. He has never talked about God or seemed to care about Him, but when I saw his eyes, I knew something good and different had happened. I had no doubt it was for real. It is like I'm married to a different man and in a good way. I don't even know how to explain." I thought my heart would burst as she spoke.

Unlike many of our guests I hated to see them go. Grant started work a couple of days later, and his boss said he was a great employee. We talked almost daily. As Christmas drew near, Missy and I knew Grant's funds were still choked from his previous unemployment, so we decided as a family to pitch in and get them some gifts.

My daughter, Kayley, voluntarily surrendered every single penny from her bank to buy something "special." Our oldest son, Lane, spent several weeks of allowance to buy Grant a ball cap for his favorite sports team after he mentioned at dinner that he was a big fan. I told Lane we were trying to focus on the kids, but he was adamant that Grant should get a present as well.

On Christmas Eve we drove over to Grant's small, over-crowded apartment to deliver gifts for everyone along with several bags of groceries. As soon as we walked in the door, the lack of gifts around their faded Christmas tree stabbed Missy and me in the heart. They were so grateful and shocked by our efforts, sincerely questioning why we cared so much.

Watching the children play with their new toys and seeing Grant's pride as he sported his new hat, which he wore cocked slightly to one side, are lingering memories that still make me smile. Most of all I remember Grant saying that year he was able to experience for the first time what Christmas truly meant. Spending Christmas with them felt so complete, everything that happened later that day seemed to pale in comparison.

Grant and I stayed in touch until the busyness of life, responsibilities, and work put regrettable distance between us. The last time we talked, he was plugged into a church and growing in his relationship with Christ and his wife. Two years passed without a conversation. I lost Grant's number when I changed phones and presumed he lost mine. A couple of times I stopped by the restaurant where Chris worked to see how everyone was doing, but I never caught her there. Even though I had not seen them, they were never far from my thoughts.

Ten months ago my phone rang, and a voice asked,

"Can I speak with Jay?" After replying that I was he, the man said, "You may not remember me, but we met at a cross two years ago. I came to your house for dinner, and you came to my house for Christmas."

"Grant! Are you kidding me? I could never forget you in a million lifetimes. I am so glad you called!"

He explained why I hadn't heard from him in so long. "I lost your number and was going through my drawer today and found the paper you wrote it on."

I was overjoyed to hear from him and even happier to learn how well his wife and kids were doing. He was still free from the issues that once tormented him. He had landed a steady, good-paying job and was being a great father and faithful husband. All the updates contained great news, but what excited me most was the one he reserved for last. It was his ongoing commitment to follow God and the positive way his life was changing. "Jay, I will never forget that day at the cross and hope you won't either!"

"Grant, listen, man, neither will I. We will literally be talking about it forever. I love you, man, and I'm so proud of you!"

Fifteen exhilarating minutes later we ended our call. Despite our promises to stay in touch, we haven't spoken since. It's OK, though. The events of that day have forged a permanent friendship between us, a bond transcending phone calls or e-mails. I continue to live in the same house where I was living that frosty December morning when I met Grant. Every time I head home, I drive past the exact field where our paths intersected and Grant found God. I can see the cross any time I want to, but usually I'm too busy looking at something else.

Chapter 3

MIDNIGHT IN AISLE SEVEN

SOMETHING ABOUT WALMART fascinates me. It may not be manly for a guy who is six-foot-six to admit, but I enjoy going there to just mill around. As much as I detest crowds when I come home from traveling, it fascinates me to watch people scurry down the store aisles as if they are in search of the Holy Grail or some other hidden treasure.

My favorite time to go is at Christmas when all of the decorations are on display and people are uncharacteristically cheery. Late one Saturday night my wife, Missy, and I decided to go to Walmart to buy some Christmas tree ornaments. As we loaded our son, Lane, in the truck and backed out of the driveway, I had no idea I was on a collision course that would take me back to the place I never should have left.

It was midnight at Walmart, and I was walking down aisle seven looking at plastic Santas and other festive gear when I brushed past a guy who looked to be in his twenties. Though I had never seen him before, I sensed something unique about him.

I quickly nodded in his direction and said, "Hello." He casually returned the greeting with a generous smile and a simple, "Hidy."

We were standing a few feet from each other, and there was something about him that I couldn't shake. I wanted to strike up a conversation but didn't want to be perceived as some kind of social vampire. My spontaneous nature got the best of me, and without really thinking through my next move, I suddenly found myself speaking.

"Excuse me, I know we've never met, and I know this is extremely odd, but I think I know something about you. I'll bet you are a Christian and that you are in some kind of ministry."

Before I go any further, let me make some things clear. I'm not one of those people who follow extraterrestrials, Bigfoot, Loch Ness monsters, or psychic hotlines. Nor do I go around harpooning people I've never met with conversation. I'm very pragmatic, but I've learned there are moments when destiny strikes and someone is placed in your path and you have to respond.

Only once before had anything remotely similar to this taken place in my life. Years earlier I was in the Atlanta airport buying some gum at a magazine store when I sensed the businessman in front of me was a believer. Although his back was turned to me, and I had not heard him speak a word, somehow I knew.

At the risk of being perceived as a stalker by the older gentleman, I struck up a random conversation in hopes of picking up some clues. Within minutes he brought up his relationship with Christ. Only then did I reveal I had approached him in hope of confirming my suspicions.

I was encouraged when he graciously told me he was glad I had approached him and that he thought God wanted us to meet. I never understood why the random encounter happened or its purpose. In fact, I had forgotten all about it until I found myself with the same premonition about the young man standing near me.

With the look of someone who had just been shot with a Taser, the man in Walmart replied, "You're exactly right! I'm Tommy, and I am the youth minister at a church in Childress, Texas. How did you know? Have we met somewhere?"

He had a hard time understanding when I tried to explain what I didn't even understand myself. I could only tell him that something in me was drawn to him and somehow I just knew.

We talked for about ten minutes, and I told him I had been a speaker to students at one time. He said that perhaps I could speak to his youth group. I gave him my number and silently prayed he would call. Not too many years before, this would have been unlikely. I had been away from God for quite some time and had only recently begun to repair my damaged relationship with Him.

The more our relationship grew, the more I wanted to serve Him. The problem was that I felt I would never have another opportunity. I was convinced that God still loved me, but I was no longer sure of much else. I wasn't worthy in the first place but certainly not now. After all, my best days were behind me not in front. Or were they? There was one way to be sure. If Tommy would call, then

I could get this settled and no longer have to live with the "what-ifs."

As we left the store that night and went our separate ways, I wanted to believe God had given me a sign that He was not through with me, that there would be a second chance. But it was easier to think this encounter was mere coincidence than dare to hope it might have been an appointment with destiny.

I would have stayed home the next day and just waited for the phone to ring if I could have, but my job at FedEx didn't permit it. For weeks the first question I asked my wife every night when I walked through the door was if Tommy had called. The answer was always the same: no call.

Six uncertain months had gone by when I happened to run into "Walmart Tommy" at a student conference. He told me he had planned to call me, but every time he thought about connecting, something had sidetracked him. He assured me that I would hear from him the following week.

I was both excited and terrified when he called the following Wednesday. As we confirmed a date for me to speak to his youth group, I did my best to conceal my nervousness. I wasn't anxious about the size of his group; I had addressed audiences much larger than this. What frightened me was the opportunity and what it represented.

I knew this one meeting would prove one way or the other if God could still use a traitor like me. As far as I was concerned, this was my last chance to find out if He had permanently put me on the shelf. That was something I felt certain of.

My nerves felt like they were being electrocuted as my wife and I drove the eighty-five miles to Childress. Tommy told me he was hoping to have at least seventy-five kids in attendance, but when we arrived, there were only fifteen or so students in the parking lot. I cannot explain how devastated I felt when I saw how few had come. I immediately interpreted this as a sign that I was an unusable castaway. My greatest fear of no longer being fit to help others appeared to be coming true.

Feeling like a death row inmate who had just been denied his last stay of execution, I told Missy, "I guess I have my answer. I told you God would never forgive me."

Fighting back the emotion welling up and faking a religious smile, I got out of the car and was greeted by Tommy, who was grinning like he knew some ancient secret. "Jay, I don't know what we are going to do, because the students in the parking lot have nowhere to sit or stand. The building is packed so full we can't even put chairs in the aisles!" I felt a rush. I couldn't believe it. Was this really happening?

I walked in, went to the front, and for the first time in five years I nervously shared the story of how years before, I began a relationship with Christ. I am not sure exactly what I said because I felt so intimidated and unworthy to be speaking. In many ways it seemed as if someone else was doing the talking.

Through the nervousness I took comfort in my awareness of God's presence. I cannot explain His nearness, but it was blatantly obvious to me and to others in the room. Then the unimaginable happened when I asked students who wanted to have a relationship with Jesus to stand. Slowly sixty-six students stood up and prayed to invite Jesus Christ into their lives. This was more than coincidence; He was clearly giving me a second chance.

One of the most frightening and hopeless feelings is to know you have made a mistake from which there is no recovery. My error wasn't intentional or calculated; it just happened. But that didn't change the results. Sometimes people, especially those in the church, can be quite unforgiving. But second chances do come, even when we least expect it. I would never have believed that a ten-minute encounter at Walmart would lead to the second chance in life I so desperately wanted but knew I did not deserve.

You are probably wondering at this point why I needed a second chance. My life got twisted five years earlier because I abandoned my faith. I quit traveling as a speaker, stopped attending church, and abandoned everything else that had to do with God. Embarrassing as it is, I must admit that when I turned away from my faith, I lived much the same way as I did before I accepted Christ.

During this wayward time I met my wife, Missy, and after eight months of dating she became pregnant. I had asked her to marry me three months after we started going out, but she wanted to finish college first. The plan suddenly changed when she found out she was expecting. We were married six weeks later.

Before I walked away from God, I had stood before numerous crowds as a speaker at schools, civic clubs, and churches. I once lived a life that led people to hope, faith, and Christ, but I became a reason for people to reject

Him. My actions spoke louder than my words, and those actions were saying all the wrong things.

On top of my guilt, regret, and shame I felt the sting of slander. Someone once said that the Christian army is the only one on earth that buries its wounded. At times I wished they would put me out of my misery. For a long time whenever I went to church, I felt as though everyone was staring at a neon sign over my head that flashed the word "sinner." I thought God was judging me just as harshly as those in the church, but I was wrong. He did not crucify me or destroy my life. He remained patient with me even as I threw away the years.

By the world's standards I had a good life. It was everything people said it should be. I was living the American dream. I had a great job with good benefits and a retirement plan. There was only one problem: I was miserable to the core. The "good life" seemed to me like nothing more than a comfortable, boring routine.

I had never bought into the idea that I should just find a good job. When I was sixteen years old, I happened upon an article in the barbershop that radically altered my outlook about work and money. One particular sentence seemed to jump out at me: "Do what you love and success will come naturally." I cut the article out and adopted that advice as my mantra. I knew if I ever wanted to really live instead of merely exist, I had to do something I was passionate about. To me that meant I had to figure out what I was called to do. I had to discover my purpose.

I was sixteen when that idea was drilled in my head, but life has a way of altering your ideals. FedEx was a great company and afforded us a steady, comfortable lifestyle. Our bills were paid, we had very little debt, and Missy was a stay-at-home mom. By all accounts we should have been satisfied, but I was burned out.

Day after busy day we were strapped into the Ferris wheel of life. We were moving fast; the problem was that we were only going in circles. Our life boiled down to fifty weeks of work and two weeks of vacation. We weren't stressed about not having enough to make ends meet, but living a purposeless existence brings its own strain.

Everyone thought Missy and I were the perfect couple. Some of our friends even referred to us as Ken and Barbie. But they had no idea of the truth. Camouflaged behind the perfect image was a couple who was just finishing two years of marriage counseling after coming danger-ously near divorce.

By the time I met Tommy that night at Walmart, my marriage was on the rebound, and I could actually say I was in love with my wife again. Our relationship still had scabs, but we were healing. I was happy with the trans-formation in my marriage but miserable with the rest of my life. I had been running from God and my purpose for so long I couldn't see a way back.

Money has never been a big motivator for me, but I always wanted to make an impact. Prominence never mat-tered as much as significance. I love people, and I have always wanted to help others. As a boy I used to tell my parents that I would change the world someday, and that was exactly what I planned to do. Somehow back then I also knew that if I wanted to do something that would last, God would have to be part of it.

But that was before I became angry with God, which led to a blame game where everyone was responsible for my problems except me. After so many years of this victim mentality I didn't know how to get my life back on track.

It's funny that even during these early years of my marriage when I was so desperate to get my life on a different path, I had no doubt that God was real. When I was in grade school I began questioning whether the God my parents always told me about really existed, and one day I decided to test their theory. I told God that if He truly was real, He needed to prove it to me by allowing me to break or hurt my right leg. (I am still not sure what made me decide upon that for my experiment.) The next day at recess we played dodge ball, and I fell on my right knee and cracked it.

My mom picked me up from school, and on our way to the doctor the pain subsided enough for me to recall my prayer. As I rode down the street to the clinic, I remember fearing God for the first time in my life—not in the way someone fears a person who might harm him—but I felt reverence and respect. Since then I have questioned many things about God, but I never again doubted His existence. But I did doubt that He would ever see fit to use me again—or at least use me as He had in the past. I had been given a wonderful opportunity to serve others and Christ, but I failed them both.

Despite this, as the years passed I found my desire to reach others grow even stronger. This is why it was with incredible difficulty that I began to face the reality that my life was not really measuring up to anything beyond a paycheck. Surely there had to be more to life than the pursuit of finances? How had I gone from wanting so much to help others to living in a mirrored capsule where everything revolved around me?

I knew the reason behind the restlessness, and I wanted to get back in line to serve God. The only time I really ever felt complete was when I was in the middle of His will, but people like me, who had made public mistakes, didn't get second chances—not from other Christians and certainly not from God. At least, that is what I thought until the night I went to Walmart and wandered down aisle seven.

One of the attributes of God's character that gives me great hope but also challenges me is that He is not predictable. He moves in and out like the wind and shows up most often when we least expect Him. I want to know that He is always present, always waiting for the perfect time to show Himself, but I am often paralyzed with doubt that He will actually show up when I most need Him.

He has shown up, again and again, and yet I still question His faithfulness. I hate to admit it, but as an adult I have asked God hundreds of times for a sign or a miracle. Most of these petitions are due to my impatience or lack of faith.

Usually the sign never comes, because God knows if He gave me a sign, I would just ask for another so I could be sure I wasn't hallucinating or that it wasn't just a coincidence. He knows me too well. I know He is not only concerned with what I do but also with when and why I do it. What appears to be a spontaneous and unpredictable move by God is actually the destiny He scheduled at the beginning of time. It just seems spontaneous to me, because I didn't know it was on the way.

In my office I have a picture frame that holds a paper

ticket. It doesn't mean anything to anyone else, but it's one of the tickets advertising the night I spoke in Childress, Texas. I have since addressed crowds of more than ten thousand, not to mention audiences in the millions via national television. However, if you ask me about the most significant event I've ever participated in, I would definitely tell you about the night my life was hijacked at midnight in Walmart, about a little church in Childress, and the way I experienced restoration from the God of second chances.

Chapter 4

CONVICTION

THERE ARE AT least two characteristics that show how sincerely a person believes in something or someone. The first is how long and consistently he has held the belief. The second is how much he has been willing to give up for his conviction. There are few things people believe in enough to die or suffer for. Most folks I know are still on a quest to identify something worthy of such sacrifice. To surrender your life for someone else is love in its purest form. There is a symbol for this kind of love—it's called a cross.

Crosses can be fashionable when worn around the neck but highly offensive when carried on the back. They can become lightning rods of division. Everyone stands on one side or the other, because crosses won't allow you to stand in the middle—you're either all in or all out.

Some express hatred toward the cross and work to minimize its importance and power. Others parrot its significance while keeping a safe distance from its bloody carnage, hindering them from ever experiencing its unexpected rewards. Even more have become so dangerously familiar with the cross they have forgotten what it really is. The cross is something that stands in defiant opposition to narcissistic, self-centered thinking, and makes a horrific call to come and die.

It sounds unreasonable and ridiculous to believe that in living you find death and in dying you find life. Crosses were never intended to be reasonable. To take up your cross is to surrender your life and its rights or entitlements. The price deceives many into thinking the cost is higher than the return, but every now and then someone comes along who proves differently.

A respected friend from Florida was invited to my hometown to share his life experiences in conjunction with a Christian concert tour that was crisscrossing the nation. The last two concerts I had attended featured the country crooner George Strait singing "Amarillo by Morning" and the rockers Mötley Crüe howling "Kickstart My Heart." I didn't know any of the bands that were appearing on this night, but I wanted to see my friend, so I scored a ticket.

The night of the event I hustled to get to the auditorium but ended up arriving unfashionably late. After listening to several of the bands, I was surprised to see a group of actors roll out on the stage to perform a drama. The play was geared toward the primarily teenage audience and portrayed a young guy who made all the wrong decisions. He landed in a dungeon of addiction and was looking for a way out.

The lights then shifted to a corner of the stage where

some Roman soldiers were spewing hatred. The man portraying Jesus was spot-on. He was jerked around by a vile, hardened-looking centurion and then mercilessly beaten with a cat-o'-nine-tails. It all looked so very real. Other soldiers mocked Jesus for claiming to be the Son of God while yanking on His beard. As they pretended to pound the nails through His hands and feet, He moaned in sheer agony. The clanking of the hammer reverberated against the walls, then they hung Him, leaving Him to look like a pathetic scarecrow.

The last words the crucified man spoke were, "Father, forgive them, for they don't know what they are doing." As the lights turned dark, the narrator's hoarse voice boomed out to the crowd, "This cross belonged to you, but Jesus Christ took your place. Will you turn to Him in faith tonight?" The attendees were invited to walk to the stage to symbolize their decision to leave behind their unbelief and sin. Then they were given an opportunity to pray a prayer acknowledging their commitment to Jesus. I was amazed at the number of people who responded; literally hundreds went to the stage that night.

After the meeting I walked out to the corridor, hoping to find my friend. Yet suddenly a girl appeared before me. She asked out of the blue, "Hey, man, how tall are you? Are you some kind of basketball player?" At six feet six inches, I've heard this question more times than I want to remember.

The girl, it turned out, was named Sara. As soon as I began fielding her question, a friend of hers named Loren ran up beside me to compare her height against mine.

Loren's shoulder reached a little above my hip. Other than saying, "Hi, I'm Loren," she just stood there quietly, but there was something about Loren that I couldn't quite place. I could feel her staring up at me as Sara talked non-stop, and every time I looked down she just gave a big smile. Sara continued to make small talk, mostly about my height, but Loren remained silent.

Loren looked really short, so I asked her how tall she was, hoping to draw her into the conversation. She said she was five feet one and a half inches tall. I ribbed her about including the half-inch, but she said she was going to count every inch she could. After that brief exchange Loren fell silent again while Sara kept buzzing with conversation, like a weed eater, and soon two of their guy friends joined our huddle.

I found out they were all sophomores in high school and came to the concert at the invitation of a friend. I asked them what they thought of the event. Sara, of course, spoke for everyone. "It was freaking amazing!"

Everyone else nodded in agreement, so I probed a little further. "What about the drama? To me it seemed so real."

One of the boys managed to get a word in before Sara. "They were as good as the actors in Hollywood," he said. Loren, however, still wasn't saying anything.

I then asked, "Did any of you go to the stage to receive Christ?"

Everyone answered with a hearty yes except Loren. She just bowed her head. She was still standing beside me, so I bumped her with my leg and said, "What about you?"

This is when the girl I thought was shy and reserved transformed in front of me and finally opened up—like a volcano.

"There are a lot of things you don't understand. I'm not even supposed to be here. If I went forward, I knew someone might recognize me and, not being aware of my situation, say something that would get back to my parents. That would be totally uncool, since my parents think I am spending the night with her." She pointed her finger at Sara.

My confusion clearly showed on my face. Realizing I didn't understand, Loren began to explain. "I lied to my parents because I knew if my dad found out I was at this kind of concert, he would beat the lie out of me. My father is a mean alcoholic, and sometimes he hits Mom and me for no reason."

I had major doubts about her story; it seemed so incredulous. I don't know everything about teens, but after speaking in hundreds of school assemblies, I can read them pretty well. And for a man, I am usually very discerning, but I just couldn't fully buy into her story.

"Come on, Loren. Why in the world would your father care if you went to a Christian concert? That doesn't make sense."

Loren explained further. "My dad is an atheist and forbids anyone in the family from going to church or anything else that is religious. I wasn't going to risk coming tonight and getting another beating, but several of my friends were going to be here, and Sara promised that my parents wouldn't find out."

I was still skeptical as I peeled the lid back a little further. "Come on, Loren. You can't be serious. You're saying your dad would slap you around for coming here?"

Sara squinted at Loren, then she said, "Go ahead. Just show him."

Without hesitation Loren went to a nearby bench and sat down. I kept trying to read the smoke signals passing between the two girls, but I was at a loss. Understanding dawned on me when Loren grabbed her plain stitched jeans around the knee and began shimmying her pants leg up.

The instant I caught a glimpse, I felt nauseous. Her legs were various shades of burgundy, blue, and stale yellow. They looked like someone had worked them over with a cane. Once I had gotten a clear view of the brutality, Loren scooted her pants leg back down and stood up.

I wanted to vomit. Embarrassed and ashamed for doubting her, I began to apologize. "Loren, I am not sure what to say. I am so sorry. I am sorry for not believing you. I am sorry for the way your dad treats you, and I am sorry for your mom."

I then asked the boys to step away so I could talk with Sara and Loren privately. I spoke to them for some time. I learned the girls hadn't discussed the abuse with any other adults because of Loren's father's threats and her fear for herself and her mother. After much talking, we came up with a plan to get Loren some help that included telling Sara's mother and contacting the authorities.

I thought about Loren's silence when I asked whether she had gone forward with her friends to accept Christ. Of course she wouldn't risk another assault. Who would? So I said, "Loren, I don't blame you for not going up front with your friends. I wouldn't have done it either if I were you, even if I really wanted to!"

Then she said, "Jay, I have to admit when I saw everything

Jesus went through for me, it touched me big-time. I was crying and saw some of my friends making a move, but I just couldn't do it. I really wanted to, but when I started thinking about what my dad would do to me, it was like I was paralyzed—"

"Loren, don't feel guilty about it," I interrupted. "I don't blame you one bit!"

What happened next I will never forget as long as I live. Loren looked down and picked at her fingernails. "No, Jay, that's not all. You see, when I was sitting there, I started thinking that if Jesus was willing to go through a beating for me, then why shouldn't I be willing to go through one for Him? I was so scared, and my life is so messed up, but I wanted Him in my life so bad I just got up and went anyway. I felt afraid the whole time, until I asked God to come in my life and forgive me. Then it was so odd, because I felt calm inside. It was like I felt everything would be OK."

I wanted to be sure I didn't misunderstand, "Loren, are you saying you did go forward? You risked getting beaten by your dad and went to the front so you could find out how to become a Christian?"

She wrinkled her brow and gave me a look that appeared to be asking if I thought she was crazy. Then a confidence seemed to wash over her, and she boldly said, "It may be odd to you, but yes, I thought it was worth the risk, and I'm glad I did it!"

I have never met anyone willing to pay such an enormous price for his or her faith. Sure, I've been to churches and seen people go forward to accept Christ. I have watched Billy Graham on TV and seen the thousands who have responded to his talks, but I had never personally met someone who believed in something enough to risk her life for it. It blew me away to see someone so young with such conviction.

I have heard it said, "You haven't found something worth living for until you've found something worth dying for." Never in a million years did I think my hero would be a sixteen-year-old girl!

Without asking permission, I grabbed Loren and hugged her tight. "I am very happy for you, and I admire your courage," I said. "No matter what, I will never forget you."

We exchanged contact info and one more round of hugs before she turned to leave. Even though Loren then walked out of my presence, I continually see her face in my memory. I wish I could see her again in person to let her know how her faith has inspired me on some of my darkest of days. When life seems to be beating me up, I remember her and continue the fight.

If I never see Loren again in this life, I feel absolutely certain our reunion will happen on a special and sacred day. Although there will be an innumerable mass of faces in that crowd, I can guarantee you one thing. I will be looking for one face, that of a courageous girl who knows what it means to take up a cross.

Chapter 5

THE ULTIMATE BETRAYAL

THE ALARM CLOCK accomplished its job. I was alarmed not only because I overslept but also because I might miss my flight. My day would be hectic, as I was flying into a major metropolitan city to speak at three school assemblies. Now that I was already running late, I'd have to fight traffic and run through airports in *two* cities, not just one. I wasn't even fully awake and the day's responsibilities were already overwhelming me.

Several frustrating hours later my flight landed safely at my destination. A friendly man who had been charged with making sure I arrived at my engagements on time greeted me at the airport. He was a sharp guy named Mark, who seemed to have it all together. He was young, married, and, based on his appearance and vehicle, seemed to be doing well financially.

We drove quickly to our first high school, where I was to tell more than fifteen hundred students about suicide prevention and the perils of substance abuse, promiscuity, and bullying. I spoke for thirty minutes; then after I dismissed the crowd, I stuck around a bit longer to talk with a group of teens who had gathered to meet me. A striking blonde seventeen-year-old girl stood out from the crowd and asked if we could talk privately. As soon as we removed ourselves from the mass of students, she sat down beside me and quickly dissolved into tears.

Like many of the students I regularly encounter, she came from a broken home. Her father bailed out on her and her mother when she was just a baby, which led her on a quest to find the love and approval she never got at home. Regrettably, in this lonely search she gave her body to several guys who weren't interested in her heart. Her reputation at school of being "easy" brought an array of guys who thought any date was a license for sex.

Twelve weeks prior to my arrival at her school she went to a football game, where her façade came crumbling down. When the Friday-night lights above the turf quit burning, she left to meet a guy she had been casually dating. She sobbed as she told me how this newfound "friend" had savagely raped her. As we talked, a close friend of hers came and sat near her as this injured girl described the lingering shame, the ensuing court case, and the other painful fallout from this experience.

This story of abandonment and the devastating effects it has on victims is one I often encounter. My heart broke for this girl and all she had endured in her young life, but I was soon to hear another story that would put the issue of abandonment in a whole new light.

After talking with this precious girl, I swiftly jumped into Mark's car to get to our next engagement on time. He was super eager to know what the students had to say, but he was particularly interested to hear about the young blonde girl. Mark had a special concern, stemming from the fact that he graduated from the same school.

Mark listened intently as I unwrapped part of the story and gave my opinion about the carnage being unleashed on this girl because of her father's abandonment. He didn't utter a sound, but my words appeared to be agitating him. Several times he nodded his head back and forth as if in disbelief; sometimes I saw him grimacing. The more I talked about this girl, the more he seemed troubled until the cork finally popped off his bottle of thoughts. Initially he seemed calm and reserved, but the longer I went on, the more animated he became. The next thing I knew, he began to pour out his own pain.

Mark was a smart, polite southern boy raised by his grandparents in a middle-class home. He made good grades, obeyed authority, stayed out of trouble, and had a strong work ethic. At the age of thirteen he followed in the footsteps of his grandparents, whom he loved and admired, by committing his life to God. He made every attempt to live a life that would honor Him and avoided many of the ditches teens often fall into. He graduated from high school then went on to college to earn a degree in accounting and make his mark on the world.

One typical college night he visited a pizza parlor, where his world collided with a fiery redhead named Tara. She was sixteen and still a cheerleader in high school. He was twenty-one. Mark said he felt "mesmerized" when mutual friends introduced them. A couple of days after they were introduced, she stopped by the sporting goods store where he worked. Before long a telephone relationship was blooming, and he stopped by to ask her father if they could date. Despite the age difference, her father was accepting, partly because he had casually known Mark's grandfather.

Tara grew up in a home where church attendance was mandatory anytime the pastor opened the door. Her parents were good, honest people who had been faithfully married for years and got along extremely well. Tara's dad was a deacon, but their faith didn't make it to the front seat. Church wasn't much more than a weekly obligation and seemed to have little to no relevance in Tara's life. Going through the motions of religion and feeling disconnected from her parents may have contributed to what Mark described as Tara's rebellious, self-willed nature. Trying to live up to a standard that doesn't represent who you really are or want to become can be very frustrating.

Before long they both gave in to temptation's pull. This level of intimacy changed the relationship drastically, and Mark found himself entangled in a web he didn't want to flee. A few months later the ecstasy turned bitter when Tara's dad cornered Mark to let him know he was aware they were having sex. Her father said he considered calling the police since Tara was still a minor.

Mark's voiced cracked as he recalled the conversation. He said he would never forget the words Tara's dad spoke that night. He said, "Mark, I want you to forgive me for planning to have you arrested. I know you can't forgive me if I am unwilling to forgive you. Mark, I trusted you with my daughter, but I have already forgiven you for betraying that trust."

To Mark, these words were like thunder before a cleansing rain. He knew his actions were wrong, but he hadn't thought through the enormity of the consequences. He knew he owed Tara's dad a debt he could never repay. What he didn't realize at the time was that a new bar had been set in his heart. Tara's dad had set an example of forgiveness he would eventually be challenged to follow.

Forgiveness has an innate power to do strangely miraculous things. Unforgiveness, on the other hand, operates like a terrorist. It plots death while masquerading as a friend. The quickest way to grow old, hard, and sick is to refuse to forgive yourself or someone else. Withheld pardon never damages anyone as much as the person who is unwilling to grant it!

Forgiveness can bring dead things back to life and restore relationships. The difficulty lies in the fact that the people we love the most always have the greatest ability to hurt us, making them the hardest to forgive. This is the reason many people have issues with trust and avoid the meaningful relationships they need most. True forgiveness is to set someone free and cancel his or her debt to you. The surprising revelation is that the person who ends up being freed is not the offender but you.

A few years ago I was devastated by the betrayal of someone who meant very much to me. This person's dishonest and cutting actions crushed me in a way I had never considered possible. This dark cave is where I learned that the ability to forgive was not something to be found but something to be chased. It had to be an intentional act of my will, where each step of healing would be paved by a previous step.

On top of the resentment and blame I felt toward the offender, I piled just as much anger toward God. I decided God must carry some responsibility since He knew it would happen and didn't prevent it. After all, wasn't He supposed to be in control of everything? I continued to ask why, but it brought no answers or healing. After a long time of letting my anger fester, I realized I not only needed to forgive the person who hurt me, but I also needed to forgive God for allowing the hurt to take place.

It seemed odd at first, because I had never heard anyone confess a need to forgive God. I grew up in the South where people don't talk about being angry with God let alone needing to forgive Him. But one day, when I was totally broken and home alone, I screamed at Him from the top of my lungs and told Him exactly what I thought of Him. I screamed that He betrayed me—stabbed me in the back—and I wasn't sure I could ever trust Him again. Even though I feared He would strike me dead, I reasoned that since I felt this way, I couldn't make matters any worse by speaking my sentiments out loud.

I came to understand that not only did God not despise me and was not going to kill me, but He could also handle me feeling He had let me down. I further concluded He was not to be blamed for someone else's actions. In time I also found out He could turn my sorrow into something beautiful and healing. As Mark continued, I remembered my dilemma and wondered if he had come to a similar conclusion. After three years of dating, Mark and Tara were married. She was nineteen, and he was twenty-four. They settled into a nice apartment and decided to wait at least three years before having kids so they could stash away some of the income he was making as a certified public accountant. Within a couple of years of marriage, two events merged to create a perfect storm. First, Tara gave birth to their firstborn, and second, Mark's sister moved in. She was a bona fide party girl who was young, single, and rowdy. Before long Tara began spending an excessive amount of time with her sister-in-law at night-clubs, dance halls, and bars.

By now Mark had taken a better-paying job working the night shift as supervisor at a chemical plant, which made it convenient for Tara to hire a sitter and cut loose, oftentimes without Mark's knowledge. Hanging out with women who didn't have the responsibilities of husbands or children began to give Tara a sense that her freedom had been stolen. Wrong communications always corrupt good manners. Mark's pleas for Tara to abandon the drunken nights and stay at home with their son were met with resentment. Even when Mark's sister moved out, the partying lifestyle and wild friends she had brought into Tara's world remained.

The turbulence settled down three rocky years later after Tara gave birth to a beautiful baby girl. The new addition settled Tara's restless heart, and Mark felt their marriage was in a great place. Tara wanted them to spend time together as a family and had no interest in walking down her old paths. For the next few years the marriage progressed well. And with a boy and a girl it seemed their family was complete. Sure, there were occasional fights and common marital challenges, but Mark felt sure he and Tara were on the road to their "happily ever after."

Five years into their marriage, without Mark's knowledge,

Tara took it upon herself to discontinue taking birth control. She had wanted another child, but Mark wanted time to weigh all the options. He was temporarily angry when she became pregnant but not because he didn't want another child—it was because of Tara's dishonesty. Nine months later when she gave birth to their third child, they both were elated.

By this time Mark was making good money and moving up the corporate ladder. He was in a managerial position, and they were living a privileged lifestyle, but something was wrong in Tara again. The children were five, eighteen months, and newborn, and her responsibilities as a mother began to feel overwhelming. Tara said she needed a break and began revisiting some of her old hangouts. She also befriended a woman who was unapologetically unfaithful to her husband.

Mark vocalized his concern that her friend's cheating ways could affect their marriage, but Tara responded in anger and accused him of making yet another attempt to control her life. He also detected in her an unusual thirst for attention from other men. At her wit's end during an argument, Tara revealed that she had been having an affair. Apologetic and remorseful she promised to stay faithful. Mark, wanting his family to remain intact, accepted Tara's promises at face value, and in time life seemed to be running pretty smoothly again. Mark was unaware of any further problems in their marriage and remained unsuspicious of Tara's actions until the pillars of supposed truth began to crumble.

Mark's best friend was a childhood buddy who lived a few houses down on the same block. This friend was in the midst of a painful divorce, and Mark spent a lot of hours helping him to cope. One afternoon Mark dropped by his home at an unusual time to see his wife. When he walked in the house, Tara decided to come clean and revealed she had been sleeping with his friend. Mark said the betrayal, hurt, and anger absolutely crushed him. After Mark calmed down enough for him to reason, Tara revealed she no longer loved him and was guilty of several other affairs. She also told him she was leaving him with the kids so she could live the life she was robbed of when she married so young.

Betrayal brings out strange things in people, and seldom are they good. As Mark told me the story, his pain could be heard, seen, and felt. This was a sad but familiar story, or so I thought. I was fairly certain I knew the outcome, and I was already speculating on how the relational doors closed when Mark threw me a curveball. "Jay, I begged her to stay, but she wouldn't do it!"

"Begged her to stay?" I replied. "You must be joking."

His answer completely stunned me. "I loved her and told her I wanted to work it out!"

Tara determined to get a divorce and moved out. Before long she was neck deep in the drug culture and completely disconnected from Mark and the children. Fearing for the safety of his children, he sought sole custody of the kids. Shortly after divorce proceedings began, Mark and his lawyer were walking into the courthouse when the attorney mentioned that she was confident they would win the case. When he inquired why, she explained she was going to expose the depth of Tara's unfaithfulness and substance abuse. Mark then made an unheard-of request for someone in his shoes: he told the attorney he didn't want to expose anything negative about the mother of his children despite her multiple affairs! He told his attorney, "I still love her, and maybe someday we can still work it out."

When I asked Mark how his lawyer responded, he said she thought he had lost his mind. When the judge evaluated the evidence, much of which had been concealed, the case was a slam-dunk, and Mark won sole custody of the kids. Around the same time their custody case was finalized, so was the divorce.

It made no sense to anyone else, but Mark remained deeply in love with his wife. Tara was furious when he told her so and made it clear she would never be open to getting back together. Tara had little to do with him or the kids, and he was constantly hearing salacious reports around town of her substance abuse and wild escapades. She never denied these claims and appeared to enjoy the hurt and concern it caused him.

While he raised the kids, she continued raising hell. She then began dating someone Mark called a "decent man." This man helped Tara settle down, and soon after the two were engaged, she became pregnant.

Five months into her pregnancy, Tara stopped by to see Mark and told him the unthinkable. She said she wanted to get back together as a couple and a family. Mark's Christian friends said he should work it out, while his non-Christian friends advised him to move on. It really didn't matter what anyone said because Mark had already made up his mind. "We definitely had problems, but the least of them was the fact she was pregnant with someone else's child. I told God if He brought her home, I would be willing to accept whatever came with her." Mark then proceeded to extend to Tara something few men would offer under the circumstances—forgiveness and reconciliation!

Tara moved back in, and Mark promised to unconditionally love and accept her and the baby. Within months, they were remarried, and he was elated. Mark paused at this point and sternly told me, "I was very excited about having another child and determined from the start the baby would be treated as though it were my own. The day that boy was born, I was the one who cut the umbilical cord, and I couldn't have loved him more or felt greater pride in someone. To this day I love all four of my children, but there has always been a deep connection between that boy and me. My son has a relationship with his biological father, but I will always be his real dad!"

Within a few months after the baby was born, Tara dealt Mark another blow. She said she never really loved him but came home because he was a better provider. She just wanted a meal ticket and a roof over her head. It was unimaginable after all Mark had put up with to think Tara would abandon him again. After a long hesitation, Mark struggled to explain how he felt in that moment. "I promised for better or for worse, but this had to be the worse. I wanted to leave, but I couldn't do it, because I knew I would never see the baby again. Custody of 'our' newborn belonged to Tara and the biological father. I couldn't bear to be pushed out of his life. I knew that would be Tara's intentions."

Few things seem to scar worse or leave more feelings of unworthiness than abandonment. It often makes people erratic, scarred, and delusional—something (or someone) they didn't know they had the capacity to become. Like vacationers in Las Vegas, they do things they would never dream of doing ordinarily. The feelings that come when one is abandoned are like the smoke of a campfire—they continue to follow you no matter which direction you move. But Mark was unmovable. To him there was only one thing left to do, and that was to stay put and beg God for a miracle.

I soaked in the things Mark told me that day. I had never met anyone like him, and his story left me feeling like I had been hit by a bus. I couldn't understand how he could love someone so deeply and be willing to set aside so many offenses. I wondered if he might be crazy or delusional. I also couldn't comprehend how Tara could behave so cruelly. I reasoned she didn't deserve Mark's forgiveness or a second chance. However, after thinking about it most of the day, I recognized I was a lot like Tara.

I had treated God the same way. I had been unfaithful to Him, abandoned Him, made promises I never kept, and, worst of all, I had done it repeatedly for my entire life. I was also like the child Mark took into his home. Even though God had no obligation toward me, He gladly made me His own.

It was pretty sobering when I contemplated that God might have allowed me to meet Mark so I could see what unconditional love looked like in the twenty-first century. This is how God felt about me. He didn't just tolerate me—He loved me completely, despite everything I had ever done to hurt Him. He would never abandon me, even if I left Him, and He would always welcome me back home if I would simply return.

Two days later I was scheduled to speak at Mark's church. At the conclusion of my talk I heard a woman wailing so loudly it sounded like she was being tortured. I wondered who she was and what could be going on. Never before or since have I witnessed anyone so completely and genuinely broken. Even though I didn't know her, I was riveted with sympathy for the woman.

Someone gently escorted her from the room, and as soon as the service was over, I anxiously inquired about what had happened. I was told it was Mark's wife, Tara. She wanted to be forgiven and have a relationship with God, Mark, and her family. That day Tara prayed for Christ to come into her life.

I met Tara that unforgettable morning and offered some encouraging words. I told her I would be praying for her and that it would be beneficial for her to press forward instead of looking back. There was radiance in her face as she wiped away her tears. She gave me a hug and walked away.

It has been two years now, but it feels like yesterday. I called Mark a couple of weeks ago to ask if I could share their story in this book. After checking with Tara, he called me back not only to give their approval but also to express their excitement in knowing their story might give others hope. Although I have not seen Mark or Tara since that weekend, I have thought about them countless times.

To me Mark still remains a most incredible example of forgiveness—a man of great character and faith. And Tara? Mark says she has been a completely different person since that Sunday morning. She is the faithful, loving wife and mother he always believed she could be. Mark is convinced, as am I, that his great forgiveness has brought him a great reward that otherwise would never have been possible.

Chapter 6

MONDAY NIGHT FOOTBALL

I WAS MISERABLE. I hated my job so much that as soon as I got off work, I immediately began dreading the next day. Two things helped me keep my mind off the monotony. The first was Monday Night Football. Watching smash-mouth warriors fight to be the gods of the gridiron on a one-hundred-yard battlefield (especially if those warriors wore silver and blue armor with a star that fell from the heavens on their helmets) helped me shift my mind into neutral and escape thoughts of work. The other sedative was nursing as many cold ones as I could drink without Missy thinking I'd had too many.

Even on vacations I could enjoy only the first three days, because I couldn't stop thinking that it would end in another four. It wasn't the job as much as the fact that I was doing something I knew wasn't my purpose in life. I was working for a Fortune 500 company that has been ranked among the top ten places to work in America. I wasn't a high-level executive; I was a delivery driver, which made the blistering Texas summers especially brutal.

Most of the trucks didn't have adequate air conditioners, and the ones that did never really cooled down because we were continually stopping. The back end of the metal trucks had no ventilation, so they often reached about 120 degrees. It was hard but honest work. I made enough money for Missy to be a stay-at-home mom, so the pay was pretty decent. We knew we would have to sacrifice some material comforts for her to stay at home, but we both felt it was a worthy exchange.

Besides the financial benefit, the job wasn't fulfilling and left me feeling I wasn't contributing anything to the good of society. I wanted more than a job; I wanted to make a difference. Although some of my misery was a result of my work, the real problem was a much deeper issue that stemmed from a detour I took years before.

Four years before I met Missy and three years before I took the delivery job, I had a life-changing encounter with Christ, and my entire focus began to change. Although I always thought I would be like my father, a businessman who owned his own company, I began to envision living a different kind of life. My initial desire to be successful was based solely on my desire to attain possessions. After meeting Christ, my money-focused vision lost its appeal. I had a new fire to do something that would last beyond my lifetime. I wanted my life to help others.

Just months after this realization I was traveling all over the United States speaking to secular school assemblies, business lunches, sports teams, Rotary clubs, conferences, and churches. Reaching people, mainly the younger generation, and helping them escape some of the same ditches I had fallen into and showing them the path to a new and meaningful life became my consuming passion.

I was twenty-two, living my newfound dream, working with and around some nationally known organizations, and naïvely thinking that anyone who called himself a Christian was the real deal.

Yet after three years I became disillusioned with the inconsistencies and hypocrisy I was seeing in many of the people I previously admired. I also began to see some of the same hypocrisy in myself. It was shocking to come to grips with the truth that many of the "Christians" I knew and worked with were some of the most dishonest, unkind people I had ever met. I walked away from what I believed was my calling, broken, discouraged, and irate with God.

Regrettably I began to climb back into the traps I once escaped from. After quitting my calling, I spent several months asking myself, and God, the why questions. When the answers did not come quickly, I gradually began to take steps away from God, mimicking what I felt He had done to me. Around this time I began dating Missy and took what I thought would be a temporary job with the delivery company. I figured I would work there for six to nine months, clear my head, and then get back to my real purpose. Unfortunately for Missy I was drifting into a spiritual rebellion that would gradually reach its peak just in time for our marriage and the birth of our firstborn.

Being newlywed and expecting a child left us little time to settle into our new life as a couple. After we married and Missy moved in, everything changed so fast, even little things. My apartment had been decked out in nothing but mallards. I had a duck shower curtain, soap dish, trash can, bedspread, and even an awesome framed print. Missy wasn't impressed. One day I came home, and it had all disappeared. I never saw the ducks again!

The marriage, the pregnancy, and all the changes these things brought were overwhelming in themselves. But added to that was the eighteen-wheeler full of toxic personal issues we had brought into the marriage. For some reason the baggage we had never addressed in our individual lives took center stage once we were married.

Missy's stemmed from being sexual abused by a family member; mine came from the misery of not living out my destiny and nursing a growing resentment toward God. Even though we had some good times, on many days we were either having a verbal boxing match or spending hours in silent distance. Most of the issues we fought over were not even the real problems, only symptoms of them.

We never laid a hand on each other, but both of us were responsible for breaking a few dishes, a window, and even kicking a hole in the wall. Immature and impatient we didn't know how to resolve our conflicts with reason, but there was no doubt we loved each other and wanted to make it work.

The one thing we never argued about and that always brought excitement was the baby we would soon have. Nine months felt like nine years. Like a mama bird Missy nested by turning the spare bedroom into a nursery. She bought matching lamps, comforters, sheets, a spinning mobile carousel, and matching wall hanging. Each item was decorated with a bear riding on a rocking horse and trimmed in baby blue. The closer we got to the due date, the crazier with excitement I became.

Late one night at around eleven thirty, Missy began having the much-anticipated contractions, so she started calling family to say she thought the baby would arrive very soon, likely that night. I sat on the sofa watching her like a prison guard and getting on her nerves by asking her every five minutes if she was ready to leave for the hospital. My mom and dad came over to our apartment, and every so often while we talked, Missy would wince and grab her stomach. I repeatedly told her we should head toward the hospital, but her mind wasn't made up. Eventually the urging of her body, my anxious questions, and my mom's insistence won out. We jumped in the truck and sped toward General Hospital.

Hospital rules were different with our firstborn than with our other children. At that time doctors were more cautious about the room being sterile. Now you can almost bring in a stray dog, but during those days I was the only one permitted. I was forced to wear scrubs, and the nurses scowled at me every time I left the room and forced me to put on a new pair each time I reentered. After eight hours of pacing the floor, calling friends, and worrying, our son Lane was born. I wanted to see every moment, and I sat behind the doctor to ensure I didn't miss a second. It was the most beautiful, spectacular, mind-bending mess I had ever seen. I felt like a rock star.

Everything about Lane was so fascinating: the tiny dimples on his fingers, his pinkish face, the stork bite on his forehead, the jelly rolls of fat on his neck, his clean smell that reminded me of a fresh snowfall, and especially the soft texture of his feet that felt like the tender inside of my Labrador retriever's ears. At the hospital I spent as much time as possible at the nursery watching Lane in his blue toboggan (which we still have) and making sure he didn't get switched with one of the other boys who didn't look nearly as cool as he did. I had heard crazy stories about babies who were accidentally switched in the nursery, and I was on guard to make sure we were not the next victims.

I spent the night on the hospital sofa and the next morning went to the local drug store to buy blue bubble gum cigars. I actually handed some out to total strangers. I also went to the jewelry store to purchase a fourteen-karat gold baby booty to put on my wife's charm bracelet. It was my feeble attempt to express how grateful and proud I was of her and our new son.

After Missy was discharged, we spent the next six days with either my mom or her mother at our constant beck and call. It was a good thing too, because Missy is tiny and her five-foot-two-inch, one-hundred-pound body had taken quite a beating from delivering an eight-pound-thirteen-ounce boy who was twenty-one inches long. Her spirit was high and joyful, but her body was tired and sore, like someone who had just been released from a prisoner of war camp. It took weeks for her to fully recover.

By the sixth day everyone had gone home, and we were on our own to begin this new chapter of our lives. I will never forget that first night all by ourselves. That's when we realized just how totally unprepared we were. It felt much like a flight I was on recently where one of the engines malfunctioned and we had to make an emergency landing. I experienced the same feeling of helplessness and terror our first night alone with our son. I thought we were ready, but when we faced the unknown, we realized that in many ways we were still so unprepared. With help from both our moms, we made it through...but barely.

I didn't know that once you had a child, you were no longer allowed to sleep. Lane was insanely colicky at night and would scream for hours as though someone was torturing him, even though he wasn't hungry or in need of a diaper change. The stress of this every single night was unlike anything I had ever known. Physically and mentally worn down with no end in sight, wanting to fix the problem and unable to do so, I began to feel hopeless. At one point we were so convinced he was in some kind of pain, Missy took him back to the doctor, even though he had previously told her Lane was perfectly fine.

He did have a mild case of acid reflux, but this was not uncommon. Most nights Missy got up with him because she was staying at home and could rest during the day, but often she would wake me when she'd had all she could take. Sleep became more important to us than almost anything. Once Lane went down, we would have difficulty getting to sleep ourselves, because we were trying so hard to hurry and doze off before he woke up. We did some unusual things to get Lane to sleep, like turning the vacuum cleaner upside down and leaving it running all night in his room (we burned up the motors of several). We would even take him on drives at 2:00 a.m. because the purr of the engine calmed him down.

As new parents we often forced the pieces of the puzzle into the wrong place, and there were many times when we made the wrong call. The only thing I knew for sure was that it felt great to be a dad. I loved having a family, but something was missing in my life. I started running away from God at mach speed long before I was married or Lane was born, and this was affecting every area of my life, though I didn't realize it at the time.

I worked a twelve-hour shift at my delivery job that began at eight in the morning and ended at eight at night. It was a split day designed to let the drivers take a long lunch that lasted between one and three hours. The amount of freight the driver was carrying determined how many lunch hours he or she could get. Sometimes we were lucky to get thirty minutes. I would often work a half-day on Saturday or any other overtime that was offered because we needed the money. But my discontentment at this job escalated after Lane was born.

I felt stuck. I wanted to quit and do something I could enjoy, but I didn't know of any opportunities that would pay or offer benefits that were as good. I thought about opening some kind of business, but I had no specific direction or capital to get started. In time I hired someone to create a professional résumé for me. After he doctored up my experience to make it look more impressive than it was, I sent it out to some possible employers. No fish were biting. Unsure what else to do, I kept grinding on.

One of the things that bothered me most was that I felt something was missing. All my life I had longed for a child, and I felt blessed to have Lane and my beautiful wife. Yet because of my work schedule, I seldom saw him awake. When I got home at night, Missy would tell me all the new things Lane had done while I was at work. I was glad she was able to stay home to see all of his firsts but was sorry I was missing out on all the special moments I always dreamed of experiencing. I had found the golden ticket but kept showing up too late to tour the chocolate factory.

My ideas about marriage and parenthood were being systematically shattered. I had blindly assumed my life would be a series of wild and crazy rendezvous with my wife and walks in the park with my happy, giggling son. What I got instead was a tired, cranky wife and a crying baby. When real-life showed up instead of the paradise I had imagined, I began to wonder what in the world I had signed up for.

As a boy I dreamed about making a mark, living a life of adventure, or being somebody's hero. I wanted to be a man someone could respect. But I couldn't even inspire myself let alone someone else. Being an adventurous hero seemed a far-fetched idea since I had a hard time respecting myself.

Spiritually I was a wreck. I seldom went to church and prayed even less. God had become an afterthought as I lived like everything revolved around me. I wasn't the husband, father, employee, or coworker I should have been. One of the burdens weighing heavily on me was the negative example I was setting for my old non-Christian friends. Many of them were watching me to see if my life-change would last. When it didn't, I gave them another reason to question the reality of what God could do in their lives. I became the excuse for them to doubt God's power.

Years earlier I had quit hanging out at the Monday Night Football gatherings where the crew and I typically got tanked. During this frustrating, selfish season when I was away from God, I got right back into bad, familiar routines. I also carried guilt on top of guilt for letting down my believing friends. At one time in their circles I was an unlikely example of someone who could make a difference, but my behavior caused some to view me as a sellout, a Judas. At other times when I wasn't feeling so remorseful, I used their disdain as an excuse to justify my anger. After all, they were supposed to help me up when I fell, right?

My family and my spiritual mentor continued to love me and never told me I was a letdown, but they didn't have to. I knew I was, and the truth stung my heart. These friends and loved ones didn't criticize or condemn me, but sometimes I wished they would. When you hurt someone, you often feel better if they retaliate, because their kindness and mercy make you feel worse. No one, including Missy, knew how deep the river of regret ran. Like a lot of men, I didn't discuss how I felt. I didn't even like to call what I was going through "problems." Instead, when I thought about my issues, I thought of them as "challenges."

Months passed without my having any real communication with God. One day while driving during work, I broke the long silence and pleaded with God about something very important. "Dear God, I know You probably won't listen let alone answer my prayer, but I have one request: Will You please just let me be there when my son takes his very first steps? I've missed most of the firsts in his brief life, and it would mean a lot to me. I know I don't deserve anything, but I'm asking for this one favor."

It wasn't articulate, and it was a bit selfish, but it was definitely sincere. I was sure that my prayer was in vain. After all, why would God respond to a runaway, prodigal son who had intentionally veered so far from the path of grace? I was certain He had much more important things to handle, but I asked anyway.

It was the end of the first day of another mundane workweek. I got home around 8:20 p.m. Missy had prepared dinner and brought a steaming plate of food to the sofa so I could catch Monday Night Football. Fourteen-month-old Lane had taken a late nap and was awake when I came home. Tired and ready to unwind, I ignored them both.

Lane was at the stage where he was crawling everywhere. Just a few weeks earlier he had gotten to the point where he had enough strength in his arms to pull himself up to the coffee table. He would hang on with his vise grips and sidestep around the table until he ran out of gas. He had never walked forward or sideways without something to hold on to.

While I ate my dinner, he practiced his routine as I tried to recuperate from mine. As I watched the game, I noticed something out of the corner of my eye that jolted me so much I couldn't move. Without my noticing, my son had turned his back to the table and was looking me straight in the eyes. Like a high-rise in an earthquake, he rocked back and forth on wobbly legs, sticking out his stubby little arms.

Time seemed to stop for a brief moment so it could take a break and look in on this scene. When I was finally able to move, I turned toward him and held out my fingers. My son took the first three unsteady steps of his life toward me and fell into my arms. I couldn't believe it! I hugged and kissed him then screamed for Missy so I could tell her the incredible news.

I couldn't believe he wanted to come to me first. No

one could ever take that away! It was one of the most unforgettable moments of my life—the fulfillment of a dream and answer to a prayer I doubted God would ever bother to hear.

That night something ordinary became something sacred. I began to see the impact Lane made on me that night as something spiritual. I realized that I also had a Father who had been waiting a long time for me to let go of all the hang-ups in my own life and reach out to Him. Gradually I began taking my own shaky and uncertain steps in His direction. It didn't seem like He was there, but He had been there all along. Just waiting.

Chapter 7

SECOND CHANCES

J OHN REALLY DIDN'T want to go. The main reason for his
hesitancy was that he didn't want to be away from
the girl he had been dating for more than a year. He
begged for permission to opt out of the family trip, but
his dad said it wasn't optional. This would be the first
and, unbeknownst to him, the last cruise they would ever
take as a family. John dreaded the whole thing—until the
day he saw the ship. It was amazing, unlike anything he
had ever seen. It had three pools, a basketball court, several dining rooms, a movie theater, and, most appealing
of all, a midnight dessert buffet.

As soon as everyone was situated in their rooms, John's
dad called a family meeting. He explained the boundaries
then gave each of the three kids what seemed like a fortune at the time: one hundred dollars. The kids could
buy anything they wanted, no questions asked. There was
only one stipulation: at the end of the cruise they had
to return whatever they didn't spend. There would be

no saving it or taking the money back home. He wanted them to enjoy this money and spend it on something they would remember. His last bit of advice was to choose what they bought wisely, because they might regret it later if they purchased the first thing they saw then couldn't buy something they wanted more. John and his sister were cranked up about the gift and determined not to give back a single penny.

The first day John and his sister spent most of their time roaming around by themselves trying to see everything on the mammoth ship. It was like a city on water. The second afternoon they spotted a casino on board and walked right in, ignoring the signs that told them they were under age and could not enter. John had never seen a slot machine in his entire life. When he first walked in, he wondered what his mom and dad would say if they knew he was breaking the law less than forty-eight hours into the trip.

He didn't have to think long because he already knew the answer. Gambling was not only illegal on the ship, but it was also forbidden at home. Since he was in the habit of justifying whatever he wanted to do, it wasn't hard for him to convince himself this was no big deal so long as he didn't place any bets or play the slot machines. The wrong thing often looks so appealing until you get in the thick of it.

John walked around the electric environment and watched people who seemed to be having so much fun. When he saw someone getting a good haul playing a slot machine, he decided he could do the same. Having only the money his dad had given him, John knew he would have to start on the quarter machines. This way any loss would be small and easier to conceal. He wanted to be cautious but felt confident he would win. The game just looked too easy.

Initially John had mixed emotions. He was both nervous and excited. The rush of doing something forbidden can be intoxicating. Many cheating spouses have said one reason they had the affair was the adrenaline rush that came from doing something secretive and illicit. The risk gave them a temporary thrill. John had similar feelings as he thought about getting caught. Parking on the edge of this cliff was dangerous, but it also felt really good.

He and his sister worked the slots side by side, but when she began losing, she had the good sense to quit. John, however, felt an impulsive urge to keep going. His all-or-nothing personality had always made him want to go big or go home. He was about even when he decided to move up to the dollar machine. He set his limit at twenty dollars, determining he could lose that much money and still keep the truth from his father. A few dollars could have easily been given in tips, something his dad certainly wouldn't expect him to give an account for.

Within thirty minutes John had won almost two hundred dollars. He thought about cashing in, but he was sure he could win twice that much. He was wrong. Before long the wheels of his winning streak were starting to fall off. With each twenty-five dollars he lost, John kept telling himself to quit, but he couldn't find the strength to put on the brakes. Too quickly he was back to the hundred dollars he walked into the casino with. Rather than walking away, he decided to keep going, assuring himself that once he won some of it back, he would call it quits.

Soon he was down to about sixty dollars, and there

was no turning back. There was no way he could explain away forty dollars. He had to push forward to recover his losses. John experienced one of the most anxious moments in his young life when he put his last dollar in the one-armed bandit. With the wheels of the slot machine spinning and his heart racing, John quietly begged God for help. Once again he was zero for three.

John felt crushed as the realization sank in that he had blown every penny his father gave him. Finally leaving the casino, John sat down hard in a chair and tried to think of some lie to tell his father. He felt the sting of regret, both for doing something he knew his parents disapproved of and because he knew he would probably get caught. He wasn't sure which of the two realizations hurt worse.

John didn't want to lie, so he decided to tell his dad the following day he had lost the money. He feared what his dad might do if he knew the truth. Back in the room getting ready for dinner, he pretended as if nothing ever happened, but thoughts of letting his dad down weighed heavily on his mind. He loved his father and wanted so much to make him proud. But whether he told the truth or the lie, he would come up short in his father's opinion of him.

A father's influence is vitally significant. Mom may set the temperature of the home, but dads set the foundation. Fathers contribute not only to the economic stability of a home but also to their children's emotional and psychological well-being.

I've found that many fathers operate in extremes. They

are either extremely loving, kind, caring, and affectionate; or they are selfish, busy, preoccupied, and angry. This often has to do with their own upbringing. Statistics show that most men who abuse their wives or children were the victims of abuse themselves. Many men who were raised in unhealthy environments reactively re-create those environments for their own children.

When I talk with students, I commonly hear stories about negative experiences with dads. Of course, I've heard countless stories of fathers who have made enormous sacrifices for their kids, but the horror stories seem to linger with me. An administrator told me about a teen in Kentucky who was sent to the nurse to be checked for what appeared to be chicken pox. Upon further review, the nurse realized the red spots weren't from sickness; they were whelps from being shot with a BB gun.

At one of the first school assemblies I was ever part of I met a girl whose father broke a liquor bottle against her chest before savagely raping her. Another man passed his daughter around to friends in exchange for drugs.

People often have a hard time trusting the Father in heaven because their dads caused them so much pain. Since their fathers didn't love or care for them unconditionally, they wrongly conclude God is the same. Trying to gain their dad's acceptance and attention proved to be a losing battle, and they don't want to go down that road again. Maybe their dad was never around to start with. Perhaps he ran off with another woman or was nasty, abusive, or critical. Father wounds can bleed for life.

An apartment manager with beautiful blonde hair and sky-colored eyes once told me the last person she ever wanted to step into her life was another father. "Fathers are made to leave," she said. "My dad left me when I was eight; ever since I've had issues with trust. When I was twenty-one, I thought I married the perfect man who would be a great father. Within twelve months of my son's birth, he walked out on us, unwilling to even send child support. I don't believe in God and doubt I ever will. If I really mattered to Him, He's had a strange way of showing it. He is no different than any of the other father figures in my life."

Although my own dad was great and supportive, there were some years I really didn't like him. When I grew into a young adult, I thought I had also grown much wiser than my father. I didn't know everything about life, but I was pretty certain I knew more than he did. I reasoned that my dad was a good man but out of touch with my generation. With each passing year I felt more eager to launch out on my own. I didn't resent my father, but I did get annoyed with always being referred to as "Jim's son." Because my dad was a well-known businessman in our city, I felt some folks never saw the real me and looked at me only as an extension of my dad. It didn't help that I looked so much like him people could spot who I was with only a glance.

I couldn't imagine at the time how much I would one day need my dad and how close we would become when I grew older. As a father myself now I have asked my dad countless times for advice about my kids, marriage, or some life issue I was facing. He has been such a great resource for help and wisdom. There were long periods of time during my youth when I didn't seek him out, but those days are long gone. As a boy he was my authority figure, but now he is my dearest friend.

As the family left their cabin for dinner, John not only felt like he was carrying an elephant on his back but that he was also trying to hide it. It was almost impossible to keep up the ruse that he was happy and excited to be on the cruise. The following day the ship was scheduled to port, and the family would be spending the entire day shopping and sightseeing. When John's mom started suggesting they buy some souvenirs, he knew he had to make a choice: either tell the lie or come clean with the truth.

Because of John's unusually quiet behavior at dinner, his mom asked if something was wrong. He denied that anything was bothering him and tried to push down the lump in his throat with gulps of soda. But the pressure kept building. Everyone was laughing and conversing about sightseeing the next day, and John was dying inside. Finally he blurted out, "Dad, we need to talk!"

John's dad turned toward him right away. "OK, son. What is on your mind?"

The lump in John's throat seemed to get bigger. "No, Dad. I mean I need to talk to you privately."

John's voice had begun to crack a bit, so his mom chimed in. "What's wrong, honey?" He didn't answer.

His dad spoke up instead. "John, we will talk when we get back to the room."

But that wouldn't work. John knew he couldn't hold it in any longer. "Dad, this can't wait. I need to talk to you right now."

With a simple OK from his dad, the two got up from the table and headed out toward the deck of the ship. As they stood beneath the clear summer sky, John grabbed the railing. He looked away from his father and toward the silver moonlight reflecting off the water in an attempt to obscure the tears bathing his face. Barely able to talk, he began his story.

"Dad, I'm so sorry. I did something today that was illegal and that you wouldn't approve of. I knew it was wrong, but I did it anyway. You're going to be really angry and let down with me."

John tried to grab the handle of his emotions but couldn't get a grip. His dad just listened. Sobbing and trying to avoid as much eye contact as possible, John continued. "I went into the casino and started gambling with the money you gave me. Dad, I lost every single dime you gave me. I didn't want to let you down, so I was going to lie and say I lost it. I know I am in big trouble, but I want to be honest. I don't have any excuse. I hope you will forgive me."

John expected his dad to lecture him or maybe start yelling. It almost didn't matter what happened. John felt a huge sense of relief from unloading the burden. His father was quiet for what felt to John like a lifetime but was actually only a brief moment. When he finally spoke, his response left John speechless.

"John, I want you to know I forgive and love you. I respect you for telling me the truth. Everyone makes mistakes, including me. I believe you have learned your lesson, which is punishment enough. Let's just have a great vacation, forget this ever happened, and learn from the experience."

It was a relief to hear his dad didn't despise or lose respect for him, but John almost wished his father had screamed at the top of his lungs. Although it wasn't his dad's intent, John felt even worse after receiving such grace from his father. John's dad gave his son a hug that felt so safe and comforting, then he reached into his pocket and pulled out one hundred dollars.

"Son, I want you to have this."

"No, Dad. Please, I don't want it or deserve it. I wasted everything you have already given me. Just knowing everything is cool between us is good enough for me."

"I want you to have it. Nothing you could ever do can change my love for you."

With this one act of forgiveness John's father taught his son things he might not have understood in a million lifetimes. The lessons he learned that day went deeper than words and have become lessons he is trying to show his own children. His father's real-life example of restoration, love, and forgiveness primed him for a future encounter with another Father.

Years later John would remember that night on the ship as he asked God to grant him the same kind of forgiveness his dad had shown. He had wasted more opportunities and squandered every one of God's gifts. He had lied, schemed, and, like before, didn't deserve to be restored. But once again he was forgiven, loved, and embraced by a Father who was willing to give him a second chance.

Chapter 8

DADDY'S GIRL

A S FAR BACK as my sophomore year in high school I wanted to have a daughter. It seems a strange dream for a sixteen-year-old guy, but I distinctly remember wishing I had a beautiful wife and a baby girl who would look just like her. Maybe the wishes were due to my growing up with two sisters and no brother. I'm really not sure. I just know I couldn't shake the thought.

Throughout my senior year I was naïve enough to think I was ready to get married and was determined to do so as soon as possible. I was mistakenly convinced every girl I dated would be "the one," but all those relationships folded like a house of cards. By the time I turned twenty-six, I began to wonder if I would ever find a wife. Then I met Missy. Things with her were different, and I knew I wanted to spend the rest of my life with her. We were married about a year after we first met.

Recently I took a stroll down memory lane and sat in the vacant chapel where we exchanged vows. It was great to reminisce. I remembered the thrilling and mind-blowing time when she gave birth to our first child. The doctor speculated that the baby would weigh around seven pounds. As it turned out, our handsome baby boy weighed in at eight pounds thirteen ounces and was twenty-one and a half inches long.

We named him Lane Hayden. His middle name was my grandmother's maiden name and was given in her honor. For Missy, who stood only five feet one and weighed just over one hundred pounds, delivering such a large baby proved to be excruciating. I was elated with my son but maintained a lingering fear I might never have the baby girl I had dreamed of.

Five summers later Missy and I went on a camping trip to the mountains of New Mexico with my sister and brother-in-law. It would be a long trip but a great reprieve from the Texas heat. We left around 10:00 p.m. and planned to drive the entire night. On top of a long drive in a crowded truck, Missy felt sick to her stomach. We finally arrived at dawn, and just as everyone was supposed to be setting up camp, my wife and sister made the insane decision to go for a walk. Exhausted, I was pretty steamed about their departure, because we needed their help to get situated. Thirty minutes later they returned, and Missy made the odd request that she and I hike up the trail.

Are you kidding me? The original plan was for everyone to nap for a couple of hours then do some trout fishing. She knew how beat I was from splitting the drive with my brother-in-law, but no amount of debate or reason could change her mind. She wanted to take the hike. Reluctantly I gave in.

As we walked up the trail, I noticed a note stuck to a tree. I took it off and read the words instructing me where to go next. Clueless but recognizing her handwriting, I asked Missy what was going on. She just smiled and encouraged me to follow the directions. I didn't say it at the time, but I thought it was totally ridiculous and foolish to be planning a scavenger hunt at such a hectic time. But I wanted to keep the peace, so I played along and pretended to be enjoying myself.

After finding a series of notes and jaunting through the mountain, I saw something completely out of place. There on a nail in a tree hung a tiny pair of baby booties. I walked over to the tree with my back turned to Missy, oblivious to what was happening and genuinely surprised to find baby socks on a tree. "Missy can you believe someone placed these booties on a nail? That's really strange!"

When I grabbed the booties and turned around, Missy had a gorgeous smile on her face that spoke more than any number of words could ever say. I was so excited and shocked that I picked her up off the ground. When I set her back down, I put a hand on each side of her face and practically shouted, "Are you serious? You are really pregnant?" With her answer came two simultaneous emotions: an indescribable happiness and the hope we would have a daughter.

Although Missy was already pregnant and the baby's gender was already been determined, it didn't hinder me from asking God for a little girl. I wasn't sure if He would answer my prayers retroactively, but I thought it was worth a try. Since He knew the desire of my heart, I hoped He would give me the daughter I wanted so badly. I had lingering doubts if a daughter was His will or just mine, but since I wasn't positive, I just continued knocking on His door.

Missy knew how enormously important this was to me, and I continually asked her if she thought it was a girl. At one point she said I was putting undue pressure on her, and I needed to resolve in my heart to quit thinking about it. She had morning sickness. It seemed a poor name for something that lasted from sunup to sundown and made her feel as seasick as a rookie on a crab boat. I didn't want to add to her stress, so I seldom mentioned it, though that didn't change the fact that I thought about it often.

One day during lunch I was driving down the street listening to the radio with the same old songs looping through my speakers. I hit the scan button to break up the monotony, and the next station pinged with a punchy, charismatic preacher. Not wanting to listen, I reached down to press the scanner again, but before I could touch it I heard these words: "Have you ever wanted something so bad it consumed your thoughts? If it is not something that is contrary to God's Word and you have asked Him to bring it to pass, then why don't you believe Him for it? Where is your faith? It's quite possible this desire came from God! So make your move! Act on your faith!"

His words took root in me. I know people tend to take advice that agrees with their own. This is why we usually don't ask someone else's opinion if we think it will be different from our own. People want to hear what they want to hear, a confirmation. But I wasn't latching onto the preacher's statement for comfort; I took hold of it because I believed it was for me.

Someone asked a wise man, "How do you know when you're in love?" He answered by saying, "You'll just know." Certain things cannot be explained; you just know in your heart. It wouldn't make sense to some people, but I was completely convinced God had spoken to me through that man's words. I was so assured that I immediately pulled into our hometown jewelry store and custom ordered a gold charm to put on my wife's bracelet. It would be a commemoration of my belief and, I hoped, spell my unborn daughter's middle name. I ordered, in capital letters, the word FAITH.

All the way up to the day Missy went into labor, the obstetrician never told us the baby's sex. On a couple of the checkups, the doctor asked if we wanted to know, but I told him we already did. Even though I was sure, Missy had her doubts. She asked me more than once if I wanted to make it official and let the doctor reveal the secret, but I wanted to wait.

The day finally came when I heard the life-changing words, "It's time!" We raced to the doctor. Missy was already almost fully dilated. We arrived at the hospital at 6:30 p.m., and at exactly 8:48 p.m. my dream came true when the doctor handed me the baby and said, "Congratulations, you have a beautiful baby girl." I wept unashamedly. When asked what we were naming her, Missy tearfully answered, "Kayley FAITH Lowder."

My career has enabled me to meet some unique people. I have addressed inmates, businessmen, students, preachers, atheists, theologians, the homeless, the wealthy, addicts, and even professional football players. I have learned something from them all, but of all the people I have encountered, no one has taught me as much as my daughter. She sees things through a different lens than others. Her honesty, humility, sensitivity, and wit are compelling. She also has a habit of asking questions only God can answer.

One night while I was tucking her into bed, she asked me what heaven is like. I did my best to explain, but every answer only brought another question. When I told her the streets were gold, the walls were made of precious stones, and the gates made of pearl, she asked if she would be able to keep some of the jewels. (I wonder if girls are just innately attracted to jewelry.) Unsure how to reply I said, "I guess so."

She responded, "So you're saying it is like Toys "R" Us, except you don't have to pay?"

I was dazed.

Her next comment was, "I can't wait to touch Jesus's skin. I bet it's really soft!"

"You mean soft like your baby brother's?" I asked.

Kayley replied, "No, I mean like Grandma's, just not so saggy."

She had me rolling!

Another night at bedtime she again started in with the questions. It can be overwhelming for me to be in the line of Kayley's curious fire, because she thinks I know the answer to all the world's mysteries, so there's no telling what she'll ask. This night I figured her question was just a stall tactic to keep from having to go to bed, and since she was already getting good at "working me" to her advantage, I tried to shut her down. But just as I was about to leave, she snuck in a question, and it stopped me cold.

"Dad, when you see Jesus for the first time, what about Him will be the most exciting to you?"

I had to think this one through. It wasn't something I had given much thought to, but the question in her beautiful mind put a lump in my throat. I hesitated for several seconds to gather my thoughts before finally coming up with an answer.

"I would say...I want to hear what it sounds like when He says my name. Since I have been to other countries and met so many different people, I have heard my name pronounced many unique ways, but I think He will say it in a way I've never heard before. What about you, honey?"

As long as I live, I will remember every detail of our visit that night: the inquisitive, probing look in her eyes, the matter-of-fact tone of her voice, and especially her answer.

"Dad, I want to hug Him, and when I put my head on His shoulder, I want to smell His hair!"

I didn't know what to say because the answer completely took me by surprise. There are traits about my family members that endear me to them—a dimple, a laugh, a grin. Kayley saw Jesus the same way I saw the people around me whom I loved—on a personal level, as close as any friend or relative. She saw Jesus not just as a King but also as an approachable friend. In her mind not only could He relate to us, but we could also relate to Him. It was freeing for me to think of Jesus as more than a faraway, untouchable God on a throne. With a few simple words my view of Jesus had been radically altered. I just hugged Kayley and told her how proud she made me. Then I jetted downstairs to share what she said with Missy.

Kayley's questions have challenged, blessed, and sometimes frustrated me. Her intuitive understanding has forced me to rethink some of my views. What is most beautiful is that she has no hidden agenda. She just calls things as she sees them. Her words stick to me like glue because she has a way of making a point without intending to.

I am a type A personality who is driven and hungry to make my mark. Like many men, I tend to measure my self-worth by what I'm able to accomplish. However, what you do is a poor and incorrect measuring stick for who you are. People can wield great influence, succeed in their careers, and obtain power without having strong or pure morals.

America has scores of celebrities who make millions through television and music but do little to influence their world for good. I have taken to heart the advice of one of my older mentors. He told me not to live a life centered on success but one fixed on faithfulness—faithfulness to your wife, children, family, and purpose!

I was in a London suburb a few months ago, walking through a historic cemetery that is older than the nation in which I reside. While perusing the headstones and reading the epitaphs, I began to wonder what mine might say. Am I living a worthy life with eternal value? It would be a great tragedy to spend a lifetime building on sand.

I read in a book, "What matters most is not what you get from your ancestors but what you give to your descendants." I have always wanted to leave a legacy for my family, but I wasn't sure how until one day when Kayley popped another question!

It was a Saturday morning, and we had plans to go shopping as a family. I woke up late and was holding up the show. In the midst of the chaos Kayley came to me with her picture Bible and asked, "Daddy, can we read some Bible stories together?"

My first thought was, "Absolutely not," and I was just about to say it when a second thought struck a nerve. "One day your daughter will have friends she will want to spend time with more than she does you. When you take the backseat, you will remember this day and regret that you did not capitalize on this opportunity. It may not always be this way!"

Humbled by my awareness of how precious my time with her is, I said, "Sure, darling!"

Since the stories are more pictures than words, we cranked out close to ten books of the Bible in less than fifteen minutes. When she matter-of-factly said, "I'm done," I felt a deep sense of satisfaction. Then I went back to preparing for our escapade to the mall.

About twenty minutes later I was walking down the stairs, and Kayley was coming up with an uncertain look on her face. She again reeled me in. "Dad, I've got another question."

I thought, "Oh, no, here we go again!"

She said, "I was just wondering, when will they write the next Bible?"

I tried to quench the question as best as I could. "Honey, there will never be another Bible written. It's the only one."

She fired another round, "Dad, you always say anything is possible, so is it possible or not?"

Like a boxer on the ropes, I was barely hanging on and uncertain how to respond. "Kayley, I did say that anything is possible, and I was telling the truth, but I forgot to tell you of the thing that is impossible. It is impossible for another Bible to be written!"

I was hoping against hope that my answer would suffice (and wondering what planet this child came from). She folded her arms and rolled her eyes upward as the wheels turned in her head. Then by the grace of God she replied, "OK." What a relief!

As I chuckled to myself, I began to wonder where the question came from and why. We needed to get going, and even though I didn't want to provoke Kayley and walk another high wire, I couldn't resist.

"Kayley, Dad was just thinking, why did you ask me when the next Bible would be written?"

Her response overwhelmed me like a tsunami. "Because I was wondering, if they did write another Bible, would they write about us? Do we live the way the people in the Bible did?"

I sat down because I felt like I had been sucker punched in the stomach. She just stood there like a mighty oak tree awaiting my reply. After what seemed like a lifetime and through "sweaty" eyes, I gave my answer.

"Darling, this is one of the most difficult questions you have ever asked me. More than anything in this world I want my life to make a difference and to help others, like the people in your Bible. I'm sure you do too, but Daddy has to be honest and say, for me, I am not yet that kind of man. I don't like admitting it, but it's true. However, I can guarantee you one thing: I will always remember this day and think about what you said, so maybe someday I can be like one of them."

I was choked up and astounded, but Kayley had no idea of the weight of her question. She simply nodded her head and waltzed away. The rest of the day I was pre-occupied by the discussion. I began to weigh who I was and what I could do to live a life that would continue to speak after it was over. I prayed silently as we traipsed around the mall. I asked God to show me His way and to give me wisdom.

It's been five years now since Kayley unintentionally drew the line in the sand for me. Yet the memory of it and the words Kayley uttered are as fresh as the day they fell from her sweet lips. I still ask God to enable me to have a life filled with meaning, purpose, faithfulness, and lasting significance.

Sometimes I take more steps backward than I do forward, and I hate that I allow mediocrity to be so deceivingly comforting. I have a very long way to go before I could ever come close to being the kind of man God would consider writing about, and I feel pretty unsure I ever will be that kind of person. There is one thing I am sure of: I'm a lot farther down the path than I was before Kayley asked the question.

Chapter 9

GAIL, A SODA, AND A STRANGER

THE LAST TWO weeks had been brutal for me. I set aside time to get away from the busyness of my life to pray and "find" God, but He seemed impossible to locate. I am usually a very upbeat person and seldom do I get depressed, but for some reason I was feeling tremendously discouraged. To make matters worse, at the same time I was fighting the blues, tornadoes swept through the Midwest and killed hundreds. I felt guilty for being depressed, since my problems are so small compared to theirs. So not only did I feel discouraged, but also I began to feel guilty and ashamed on top of it.

Everywhere I turned there seemed to be an armada of opposition waiting to greet me. Anybody who really knows me understands I am a live wire. Very rarely do I get down in the dumps or remain frustrated for very long, but I was feeling lower than I had in a quite some time. I began to question everything about myself and my faith, and the weight of uncertainty led me to become unusually inactive. Why is it that when we are discouraged we become so lethargic?

Compared to most people I know, I have been greatly blessed. My life is good. How could I feel so bad? I have been told that when you are feeling blue, one of the best things you can do is to focus on others. I have given this advice numerous times, but I often have difficulty putting it into practice myself. Yet little did I know my own advice would lead me to encounter Jesus in a whole new way.

Around this time I had started picking up my eight-year-old daughter, Kayley, from gymnastics twice a week. Every day we'd travel a highway called Kell Boulevard. We'd drive a few miles, then turn onto Holiday Street, and drive through what local police consider one of the most dangerous parts of the city. Without fail we would always see a wrinkled old lady sitting in the grass wearing two or three coats and a cap, smoking cigarettes, drinking out of two-liter Dr Pepper bottles, and talking to no one in particular as she gestured with her hands and stared out into space.

On our way home Kayley always wondered aloud if "that lady" would be in her usual place. She is still young enough for her heart to be tender and not jaded. She typically mentioned how sad she felt about the woman and how she wished there was something we could do. One day I actually mentioned stopping, but it scared Kayley too much for me to actually do it. Her heart was saying yes, but her mind was saying no.

I probably wouldn't have stopped anyway, because I have spent enough time around the homeless to know you can get into a dicey situation if you're not careful.

Although this woman pulls on your heartstrings, there is also something about her that is scary and intimidating.

Still the woman had become a hot topic in our home, and every time the weather got bad, Kayley would wonder out loud where she had gone for shelter. Yet when it wasn't raining or when we weren't passing by the woman's usual spot, our lives went on. Even though this homeless woman would visit our thoughts from time to time and become the center of dinner conversation, I honestly didn't know what we could do. It seemed she needed long-term care from mental health professionals, something well beyond our ability.

One day I had a lunch meeting with a friend at a hamburger joint that just happens to be located on the very street where this woman had been making her home. After my meeting was over, I asked our waitress for a cherry-lime drink so I would have something to swig when I got back to the office. It is impossible for me to get back to work without driving past "the lady," and I found myself curious, as always, to see if she would be sitting in her customary place. As expected, she was there, sitting on top of a tent in a wide-open field smoking cigarettes and talking to someone or something that was not there. I could not stand just wondering about the woman anymore, so I pulled my truck over to the curb, grabbed my cherry-lime drink, and walked toward her.

It is difficult to describe her physical appearance. Common sense told me she was probably somewhere between sixty and seventy years old, but time has aged her well beyond her years. I am not exaggerating when I say she looked at least one hundred years old. Her skin was weathered like a worn-out saddle, and the blue veins on the backs of her wind-chafed hands were unusually pronounced.

I had never seen her when she wasn't sitting down, but I guessed her to be around five feet four. She was dangerously thin with faded hazel-green eyes that appeared to have clouded over time. Her eyebrows were so thin they were almost nonexistent. She wore old worn-out clothes and a pair of brown leather boots with a zipper on the side. Her bare toes peeked out the front of one shoe where the seam had come loose.

As I approached, she began staring me down like a cornered tiger. Before I came too close, she assailed me with a tongue-lashing unlike any I had ever received. The verbal assault lasted only for a few minutes, but it seemed much longer. Despite this, I never considered walking away, because something kept telling me that if I could be patient, she might eventually allow me near.

I could sense her surprise when she realized I was not going to just walk away (like most reasonable people probably would have). The woman squinted at me, took a minute to catch her breath after giving me such an earful, and finally settled down enough for me to come a little closer. When I was standing just a few feet away, I squatted down on the backs of my heels and hoped to get a word in this time.

"Hello, ma'am," I said cautiously. "I'm sorry to bother you, but I saw you sitting here with a coat on, and since it's such a hot day, I thought you might enjoy something cool to drink." I handed her the drink, and in a hateful, gravelly tone she immediately demanded to know what it was. When I told her, she snarled like an angry German shepherd and with disgust in her voice commented, "I have never tasted a cherry-lime in my life."

I sat there studying her sunburned face; the lines were so deep around her eyes and cheeks they reminded me of the ruts in a freshly plowed field. Her lips sank so far back into her mouth that their pink outline was hardly visible. Her ear lobes were split in two, as if the earrings had long ago been yanked from them. All of her worldly possessions were lying on the ground next to her, and there were no more than four or five items.

She was sporting a dirty blue baseball cap and wearing three coats despite the fact that it was over ninety degrees. When she removed her cap to scratch her head, I saw bright red hair. Everything except the curls hanging past her ears was matted down to her scalp as tightly as a woven rug. "I love your beautiful red hair," I said. She complained that it was so matted she couldn't get a comb through it and said she hadn't looked in a mirror in years. I suspected she owned neither.

As if no longer skeptical of the cherry-lime drink, she sucked on the straw like someone who had been lost in the desert for days. Then in that gravelly voice she said, "What do I owe you for this?"

"Ma'am," I replied, "you don't owe me anything. I just wanted you to know I care about you." She then proceeded to tell me if I thought she was a prostitute, then I was wrong, and in no way would she repay by sleeping with me.

"Ma'am," I said, "you don't understand. I honestly don't expect anything from you. I just wanted to offer you something to drink and make sure you're OK."

I stayed for another twenty-five difficult minutes and

just listened to her. With each passing second her skepticism seemed to fade. The longer I stayed, the more I felt that maybe she was beginning to see I really cared.

I asked her name, and she told me she was going by Gail. When I asked her age, she said she thought she was fifty-nine. At least three or four times while we were talking about something completely different, she would assure me she was not a prostitute and had never been one. Of course, I had never even mentioned anything of the sort. But since it was so important to her that I didn't think that of her, I figured somewhere down the line she may have been involved in prostitution, or it wouldn't have been at the forefront of her mind.

Through our conversation I picked up bits and pieces about her life. She was from up north and had two children. "I don't want to talk about my children," she abruptly told me. "It's too painful." She said her children didn't love or care about her, but she began to tear up when she talked about the death of her mother. The conversation was disjointed, and I couldn't always follow her train of thought. Mostly I just listened.

At one point I asked if she wanted to take her coats off, but she said she would rather leave them on so they didn't get stolen. I couldn't imagine how she functioned with three coats on in such heat, but I also couldn't fathom living in a field on top of a tent instead of inside of it.

Before I left, I asked her if I could pray with her, to which she angrily responded, "No! I hate God, and I don't believe in Him or ghosts." I decided not to press the matter but told her I would try to come back soon to check on her. The rest of the day I was so busy thinking about my encounter with Gail my own discouragement seemed to disappear.

That night was date night with my wife, Missy. We decided we would go out to eat. As we sat at a local deli drinking sweet tea, I relayed every word of my conversation with Gail from earlier that day. I could tell Missy's heart was troubled, and she told me she wished there was something we could do. On our way to dinner my assistant had called to ask if I would drop by the office to get something. It wasn't really what I had in mind for date night, but it turned out to be providential.

Since we had to go to the office, Missy mentioned that we might as well see if Gail was in her usual place since we had to drive right by that field. When we turned onto the street, I slowed my truck down to a crawl. As usual there was Gail, smoking and talking to her fantasy friends.

We didn't stop but continued on to the office and completed our errand. As we were leaving, it suddenly started to rain, and Missy wondered whether Gail was just sitting outside in the pouring rain. She suggested we drive back by and check on her again, and while we were on our way there, Missy also decided that I should ask Gail if we could get her something to eat.

When we arrived, I got out of the truck and slowly approached Gail. She was still sitting on the tent, despite the rain. I asked if she remembered me and was pleased that she did. After talking for about two minutes, I told Gail I had my wife with me. I then motioned to Missy, who was sitting in the truck, to come join us. With all three of us getting misted by the light rain, Gail said if she could have anything in the world to eat, she would like biscuits and gravy with no sausage. She said she didn't like meat, because it was hard on her stomach. And she asked for a Dr Pepper.

It was obvious that Missy's presence put her more at ease. Only God knows her wounded past, but I felt sure it was filled with corrupt men who had brought insult, shame, and injury to her. Quite frankly, as much as I wondered about how Gail ended up at this point, I was also hurt that her life seemed to be riddled with such pain.

Missy and I loaded back into the truck and drove to the nearby IHOP to pick up an ice-cold Dr Pepper and biscuits with gravy and no sausage. When we returned, Gail was both grateful and excited. We were exchanging small talk when an old truck pulled up next to mine and parked. A Hispanic man wearing a blue-collar company uniform got out and began walking our way. I couldn't pin it down, but I knew immediately there was something special and different about him. The humble way he approached with his head slightly bowed and the gentle look on his face piqued my curiosity.

Without saying a word to us, he addressed Gail by name in a voice as soft as silk and asked her why she wasn't in her tent. She told him the police had told her it was against the law. I began to put the pieces together and realized this man had given Gail the tent she was always sitting on.

As he bent down to gently tell Gail how concerned he was about her, I couldn't help but feel respect for this man. He was a big guy but as tender and sincere as anyone could be. I turned to the man and told him my name and thanked him for helping Gail. The concern never left his face.

"Every time I see her, it tears my heart in two," he whispered. Then he looked back at Gail and told her he was going home to eat dinner but would be back in about an hour to check on her.

I wish I could express how I felt toward this man. His kindness and sincerity were overwhelming. "Sir," I said, "you must be a Christian."

He answered modestly, "Yes, but not a very good one."

"That makes two of us," I replied as I thought of Gail's circumstances in the midst of a city of plenty.

The man added with a smile, "But I do love Jesus."

I wanted to hug him, but all I could do was say thanks. To my regret he then walked away, and I found myself wondering if I would ever see him again. Missy and I stayed a few more minutes assuring Gail we would be back to see her. As we drove away, I broke the long silence between Missy and me by asking her if she happened to notice the name on the man's work uniform. She answered, "Of course I did. Why do you ask?"

"Doesn't it strike you as strange that even though the man's name is pronounced differently, it is spelled J-e-s-u-s? How appropriate is that? The world may have forgotten Gail, but she was remembered by Jesus."

Missy said she hadn't thought of it in this way. Chills ran down my back.

I chuckled at the play on words and marveled that the one person we came in contact with, the one who showed compassion for the alone and hurting, just happened to have the name "Jesus" written across his chest. What are the odds? I'm convinced that as far as Gail is concerned, being near Jesus is a lot like being near Jesus. I cannot imagine that Jesus Christ Himself would have responded any differently than this man did. His reassuring voice, his warm smile, his compassionate heart and nonintimidating approach—they all reminded me of Christ Himself. He loves unconditionally with a tender heart that bleeds for the broken.

Gail showed me that you can learn a lot by hanging around people who are hurting, things you could never learn anywhere else. Unfortunately, few of us want to associate with the broken, including many churches. For the most part we don't want to be inconvenienced. I stand among the guilty.

It takes a lot of patience and understanding to help people wade through the raw sewage of pain, abuse, addiction, disease, and neglect, and sometimes I am such a hypocrite I don't want to take the time. Too often I'd rather soothe my conscience with some explanation for their suffering—that they were too lazy to work or that they gave up on life and themselves—than to give of myself and help make their lives a little better.

Jesus never responds as I often do. He doesn't turn a blind eye but chose to give His life for us despite our sin, our pain, and all the havoc we create. If we focused on remembering what He has done for us, we would have His determination to help others realize He has done the same for them. His passion to love and heal the wounds inflicted by sin was meant to become our own. You never know what might happen when you become willing to love the unlovely. It's a messy business, but there's a good chance that while you're serving, you just might run into Jesus.

Chapter 10

IOWA PARK

M Y YOUNGER SISTER, Alara, is the real deal. She has the grace and beauty of a monarch butterfly and the warmth of a January fire. When we were younger, I used to love to hate Alara because her honesty always made me look like a criminal. She was one of those people who might have been off playing the harp or feeding the poor or praying for world peace while you were busy doing everything wrong. Although my character didn't measure up to hers, I have always respected Alara because of her consistency and dedication. I knew she was what I wanted to be even when I wasn't sure that was even possible.

Even during high school and college—one of the hardest times of life to resist peer pressure—Alara took a bold stand for her faith. She walked what she talked. In street language, she was smoking what she was selling. She had an undeniable way of living life as a believer without portraying herself as a self-righteous person who had it all together. Even now she believes I give her more credit than she deserves.

Although she is a knockout with an engaging personality, her attributes didn't translate into her becoming Miss Popularity. Guys weren't banging on the door for a date, and the girls she knew were sometimes mean or distant because of her stand. Her faith cost her friendships and acceptance, but she didn't waver.

She has never been one of those obnoxious Christians who think they are always correct. Her way of living for Christ didn't involve browbeating people into submission or looking down on those who didn't share her beliefs. She was the girl people turned to when trouble hit, someone they knew really cared. If she ended up in the middle of a debate about her views, no one could ever accuse her of being hypocritical, judgmental, or hypercritical of others. Even those who didn't agree with her tended to respect her transparency.

The world doesn't trust many of the people who call themselves Christians. I don't either. The reason? Most who wear the label don't live the life. It's only a moniker. American Christianity has preached a diluted message for so long, the masses of "believers" have no idea what it truly means to be one. I have many friends who spent years thinking they had an authentic relationship with Christ only to realize later it was just the cheap substitute known as religion. I have been called many things, but no label has ever bothered me more than being called religious. I never committed myself to a religion and have no plans to do so in the future.

This polluted representation of Christianity has tainted the world's view of who we really are. It's no wonder that we are dismissed and despised. Although blame for this negative image is often placed on the media, the ones responsible are church people, church leaders, and people like me who have on way too many occasions shown judgment and condemnation instead of love. Our stand for truth may be right, but our way of communicating it can be so very wrong. Too often we show little patience, mercy, grace, or compassion, and way too much inconsistency and overconfidence to those who don't believe as we do.

A month ago I was watching a documentary about a church in Kansas that applauds earthquakes, the tragedy of September 11, 2001, and the deaths of American soldiers. They carry signs saying "God Hates Fags," "God Hates America," and "Thank God for Dead Soldiers." My oldest son watched the documentary with me. During the show I occasionally glanced over at him to see how he was responding to what we were seeing. He was as disgusted as I was. Several times he shook his head in disbelief. When it ended, he angrily said, "I can't stand people like that."

I told him, "Son, our fight is not with them but against what they stand for. We need to help others realize people like them do not represent who we are or what we believe."

Even though this ridiculous, perverted "church" represents an extremely small segment of the population, they have received nationwide exposure. It was a sobering reminder of how the world looks to see what confessing Christians will do and how carefully we must guard our actions. Most of us will never appear before millions on TV, but we cannot deny that every one of us is being watched in our own social circles. Daily.

The message we send and the example we set make a lasting impression on others' opinions of Jesus. I regularly meet people who think because I have faith I condemn those who are gay or nonbelievers, drink alcohol, play poker, dance, or go to the movies. None of this is true. I dropped my stones long ago.

After high school Alara began college, and her velvet heart was still convinced she knew someone worthy of telling others about. During government class her freshman year, she was placed in a small group for a project and met a sweet girl from a country family who was studying to be a radiology technologist. Alara's classmate was from Scotland, Texas, a small, one-horse town with no stoplight located twelve miles south of Wichita Falls. Most consider it the middle of nowhere.

Unbelievable to them both was the revelation that two days a week they were living right next door to each other. Alara lived at home with Mom and Dad and shared a fence line with this girl's aunt. On days when the friend had late classes, she would stay with her aunt so she wouldn't have to make the drive back to Scotland in the dark after work. Three times each week their cars were parked less than thirty-five yards apart, yet Alara had never seen this girl one single time. The two homes were separated by a row of twenty-foot hedges, but it still seemed remarkable.

Before long the two became very close and spent much of their time hanging out doing girly stuff together. I ran into them one day at my father's convenience store, and Alara introduced us and told me the story of how they learned they were neighbors. Some time later my sister asked me to pray for her new friend because she knew she was a nonbeliever and wanted to somehow tell her about Jesus.

Alara's new friend came from a good, country family. They were honest people who attended the local Catholic church only on the rarest of occasions. Alara's primary motive was not to sneak up and spiritually "harpoon" her classmate but to be her friend. She didn't push or prod her, but neither did she conceal her trust in Jesus. The friend appeared neither negative nor particularly receptive.

Their relationship continued to grow, and four months after they met, my sister invited her to ride along to hear her favorite speaker at an event in the sleepy little town of Iowa Park. Alara believed if your faith were a priority in your life, it would be a normal part of your conversation. Followers of Christ have gotten a bad wrap for trying to "convert" everyone. In actuality that's something only God can do, and statistics prove a very small percentage of Christians ever tell one single person about their faith.

If something makes your life fulfilling, worthwhile, or complete, it is only natural that you would share that with others. How much more when that something is your God? Can anything be more selfish than believing you have a cure or solution and keeping it only for yourself? Being pushy, obnoxious, or coercing is never right when sharing belief, but it is also wrong to be unwilling to rationally discuss matters of faith.

Much of the Christian rhetoric is misplaced; it is centered on kingdom issues instead of the King Himself. I'm amazed by how many Christians spend more time talking about the Ten Commandments being removed from their local courthouse than about Jesus. Why complain about the possibility of "In God We Trust" being removed from currency if we are not trusting God in our daily lives?

I can't tell you how many ridiculous e-mails I received last December about the need to boycott certain franchises because they were calling Christmas "the holiday" or "Xmas." Many of these same critics who lambast city leaders for forbidding nativity scenes or the posting of the Commandments on government property have never put up either in their front yards or homes. So why be so angry when others follow the example?

Boycotts don't bring people to God any more than monuments do. Unconditional love does. Protests only cultivate feelings of antagonism and resentment. If we truly want our faith to be on display, the greatest place to do this is not on the courthouse wall or the city park but in our lives. And it's done through our actions and willingness to tell others about Jesus. Our first calling is not to rescue a monument or holiday symbol but people—they are the ones Christ gave His life for. I agree that it's not enough to tell people about our faith if we don't practice it, but what good do we do if we practice it and are unwilling to share it?

If the church truly believes people without Christ are eternally separated from God in a painful, horrendous place, then why do the majority of churchgoers never attempt to divert one single person from that destination? What should bother them most bothers them least! I went to San Antonio a couple of years ago on a family vacation and stayed in one of the dozens of hotels running shuttles to the Southern Baptist Convention, which happened to be going on at the time of our visit.

Two days after arriving, a friend from Baton Rouge called and asked me to meet him at the convention. Thousands were attending the gathering, and the conference site was congested with people. After meeting my friend at the event, I stood in a long line and waited thirty minutes to jump back on the shuttle to my hotel. After making stops at what seemed like dozens of other hotels, the shuttle finally arrived at my stop one hour later. As I heard the people around me ranting in their spiritual lingo, I wondered how many were brazen enough to talk with our driver. Before I rocketed off the shuttle, I gave in to my curiosity.

"Sir, may I ask how many people you have driven today for this convention?"

He looked surprised by my question and answered, "It would be hard to say since I have been driving busses full of different people for ten hours straight, but it's been at least several thousand. Why do you ask?"

"I was just wondering. May I also ask if you are a Christian yourself?"

Chuckling he said, "No, not me, I just drive 'em around!"

The bus full of people got quiet.

"I just want to know one more thing, sir. How many of these folks have talked to you about Jesus or how you could become a Christian?"

"Not a one of 'em," he replied.

I then gave the simplest and quickest explanation of the gospel possible. A minute and a half later he shook my hand, smiled, and thanked me for caring.

Before the meeting in Iowa Park kicked off, Alara came up to say hi and to remind me that I was in her prayers. Standing beside her was the friend from her class. The girl smiled, showing off a dimple deep enough to hold a nickel, and simply said hello. Alara asked if I was nervous about my talk but told me I would do great before I even had a chance to answer. Then she gave me a bright smile and winked at me before kissing me on the cheek. I was encouraged by Alara's presence, partly because my girlfriend was unable to attend. I told my own story that night. I tried to help people see that you could believe in Jesus intellectually or even attend church but still not have a relationship with God.

No matter how hard I tried to communicate, my words felt as though they were sticking to the roof of my mouth like peanut butter. As I began to draw my talk to a close, I felt handcuffed. Before the sting of discouragement completely spread its poison, I explained how people could have a relationship with Christ, but my words seemed to have minimal impact. When the meeting was over, Alara gave me another hug before leaving and told me I made her proud. I still felt deflated but appreciated the encouragement. Before her friend walked away, she mentioned being glad that she came. I didn't know if she was just being polite. I hoped something I said had touched her, but I couldn't be sure I'd connected with her or anyone else in the audience for that matter.

Ever since I was a boy, I've been fascinated by people who found a purpose worth fighting and even dying for. When I was in junior high, I read a lot of books about Native American warriors such as Crazy Horse and

Geronimo. I was captivated by their commitment to their people and their willingness to protect them. I would often daydream about what it must have been like to have their courage and strength, and I'd imagine myself riding a warhorse on the prairie with paint on my face and a tomahawk clenched in my fist. I guess I never grew out of it because I am still enamored with people on a mission, and I find myself watching movies such as *Braveheart* and *Gladiator* over and over.

As a grown man I still want to be a part of something spectacular. I recently found myself daydreaming about how awesome it is going to be to hear David tell about his battle with Goliath, Daniel relay the details of the night he had a slumber party with lions, and Moses tell what it was like to watch the Red Sea part and crash down upon the slave-driving Egyptians.

In the fog of my musing I began to wonder, "What if they asked me to tell about all the supernatural things God did through my life? Would I have anything to share, and if not, why?" Then I began to pray, "God, please don't let me go through life without being a part of something supernatural. Let me live life in such a way that I will have something to tell David, Daniel, and Moses."

Maybe that's why after becoming a Christian I assembled a group of friends from college to walk the streets downtown to hand out tracks, feed the hungry, and talk with people about Jesus. I was bothered that most students who would readily attend Bible studies were uninterested in talking with the hurting and forgotten. One of the guys who went out with us became my brother-in-law. Our group had some amazing, miraculous, and sketchy times together talking with strippers, drug addicts, drunks, gang members, and the homeless.

Some of the best and most memorable times of my life were on those prostitute-riddled streets. One time we walked under a bridge around midnight to help out some drunken winos who had been nursing bottles of Thunderbird all day. As we approached, the reflection from their campfire revealed a zombie-like figure waving a rusty old revolver in our direction. His voice sounded like tires on loose gravel as he threatened to "put us out of our misery."

Common sense says you do not try to reason with a drunk, but we had given up "common" sense a long time before. Instead of doing the smart thing and leaving, we raised our hands as if in surrender and asked if we could sit by the fire and talk. The man with the gun let us stay, but we didn't stick around for long, because it was clear he had a lot of gun and very little ability to reason. He had less sense than we did, which says a lot.

We were downtown so often that many of the girls hooking knew us by name. I'll never forget the first time a small group of prostitutes saw us coming and rushed away. I didn't understand why they would avoid us, and it hurt my feelings. The next time I saw them I asked why they left so quickly. They explained that they had no issues with any of us, but their pimps would beat them if they didn't make a certain amount of money.

Numerous times people approached us to ask for prayer, and we saw things happen I never thought possible, some of which I have never seen since. Like the night a biker came out of a topless club so drunk he could barely walk. I initiated a conversation, and he started talking about his mom and how she had prayed for him for years. I silently prayed that God would sober him up so he could grasp what I was saying, and within minutes he was as sober as Mother Teresa. He ended up on his knees in the parking lot, crying and asking God to forgive him. When he left, he promised to call his heartbroken mom to tell her he'd made things right with God.

The only people who really despised us were the men who hovered at the porn shop. In those days it was called a peep show because men went inside small rooms where they deposited quarters to get a "peep" at nude films. They didn't avoid us because we hassled them; they just wanted to camp in private.

Our adventures were dangerous and thrilling. When I took some of the homeless who hadn't bathed in weeks to church, I thought some of the blue hairs (the elderly women whose gray hair for some inexplicable reason was always blue) were going to have a stroke. Even though I often didn't share my faith the right way, I knew that being unwilling to share it at all was always wrong.

The night after my talk in Iowa Park, my sister called crying. She said her friend called her after she arrived at home to tell her that during the service she realized she had never put her trust in Christ. On the drive back to Scotland she was thinking about what I said about Jesus dying on the cross and had to pull over her car because she was so broken. Feeling convicted over her rejection of Christ, she began to ask Jesus to forgive her and come into her life. Alara was on fire with excitement as she relayed the details. I was amped too as I listened to how God had captured this girl's heart.

Sometimes I wonder what would have happened if my sister had not been willing to get out of her comfort zone and risk losing a friendship. Would this friend of hers have ever accepted Christ? Would she have been eternally separated from God? Would any other believers have told her about their faith? Or would they have told themselves, "It's not my business or responsibility"?

Did anyone else care about this girl's destiny, or would she have only come in contact with those who excused themselves by saying everyone has a right to believe what they want, without even trying to amicably sharing the truth? I don't know all the answers to these questions, but I do know this: had my sister not stepped out of her comfort zone, her friend might not have ever become a believer—and she might never have become my wife and the mother of my three children.

Chapter 11

DYSFUNCTION JUNCTION

TORI WAS A talkative, attention-craving daddy's girl. She was born with auburn hair—reddish brown like a sunset in a dust storm—fearless blue eyes, and a bold habit of speaking her mind. Her ability to take any party to the next level brought her just what she wanted: an abundance of friends. She longed to be recognized, liked, and accepted—desires that likely stemmed from the fact that she was adopted. Something about being given up by her mom made Tori feel less than others, that she must not be worthy or deserving. The venom of rejection coursed through her being.

Tori had known from the time she was a child the people she called Mom and Dad were not her biological parents. What she didn't understand was why her biological mother didn't want her. Whether her mother really felt that way no one knows, but Tori was convinced it was true. Again and again she asked her adoptive mother, "Why did my mom give me away?" The answer was always the same, "Your mother was sixteen, unmarried, and couldn't provide for you." No matter how many times she heard those words, they never brought the reassurance she longed for. Tori often pressed the issue, because she knew each time her parents would wear down a little more and reveal a few more pieces of the puzzle.

In time Tori learned that her birth mother, Sarah, wasn't allowed to contact her, because those were the terms of the adoption agreement. Tori didn't have a say in this pact, and she determined this would not stop her from trying to find her birth mother. She was convinced her search would reveal not only her mother's identity but also her own. Yet no matter what she did, the closet full of secrets seemed impossible to open. That's mostly because Tori's parents were determined that she never find the key. In their opinion, some truths were better left untold.

Kate and John were typical middle-class people who adopted Tori as soon as she was born. Kate was a secretary, and John worked as a highway patrolman until he found a new career as a company man. He managed money well, possessed a great work ethic, and consistently moved up the corporate ladder. He wasn't an affectionate man, only telling Tori he loved her on rare occasions, but she knew how he felt. She was especially convinced of his devotion when he bought her a very expensive flute her mother said she couldn't have. This one act convinced her she was something special in his eyes.

John was on the city council, a member of the country club, and very good at hiding his alcoholism. At night he would look at porn, drink too much, and take his frustrations out on Kate, but he never mistreated Tori. For sure he was a strict disciplinarian with high expectations for Tori, but he was never excessive. She loved him dearly and, like many daughters, had him wrapped around her finger.

Kate was another story. By the time Tori was seven, Kate had given birth to two children of her own, and she didn't have any problems showing them favoritism. From the outside Kate was a good, churchgoing mother of three. The view from inside told a different story. Kate was negative, cranky, critical, and way too concerned with putting on a good face for the people who mattered the least: outsiders.

Tori spent her childhood moving from city to city. John's promotions required it. For a girl with insecurity issues, being on the move only made matters worse. Despite the unsteady bridges, Tori earned good grades, played in the band, performed in plays, and generally excelled at everything she tried. But her growing list of accomplishments did nothing for her self-esteem, especially since she was heavier than most girls her age.

Tori desired love and affection so desperately she was willing to get it any way she could. She was only in the sixth grade when she French kissed a boy while playing Truth or Dare. By the ninth grade she had given her virginity to a nineteen-year-old, whom she broke up with the following week after she saw him with another girl. The breakup left her heartbroken and tearful for days; its effect on her outlook on life would last much longer. Feeling devastated and used, she concluded she wasn't worthy of love.

In high school she became a magnet for all the wrong guys. They didn't have to seek her out; she sought them. In her mind she didn't deserve any better. One day one of the boys forced her to have sex, but she didn't tell a soul. She was sure nobody would believe her allegations, because she had been with so many guys. At one point she began dating a good guy who never pressured her for sex. He was kind and compassionate, someone Tori thought she could marry someday.

Everything felt so right, at least until a drunk driver killed him. It was the final straw. Tori decided she was done with God. She was done with His unfair way of permitting people to leave her, and she was done allowing herself to get too close to anyone who might walk out on her or be taken away.

One summer break while she was in high school, Tori and her family attended a family reunion. A cousin asked Tori if she knew who her mother was. Tori told her she didn't know anything about her except that her name was Sarah. The secret her parents kept wasn't hidden among Tori's extended family. This cousin knew exactly who her mother was—her last name and even where she lived. She had even been a babysitter for Sarah's kids. If Tori were interested, she could let Sarah know Tori wanted to meet her. Days later Tori received a call at work: "Victoria? Hello? This is your mom."

Being called by her full name, something no one else ever used, made it stunningly clear who the caller was. For the first time in her sixteen years Tori heard the voice of the woman who had given her life. The conversation was brief. Sarah would be passing through town in a couple of weeks and wanted to know if they could secretly meet. Without hesitation Tori agreed, choosing the local Dairy Queen as the meeting place.

Tori had been grounded from driving because she had wrecked her dad's truck, so on the day they were scheduled to meet, Tori made the heart-pounding, clandestine journey on foot. When she walked in the door, Sarah was standing there waiting. Tori's first thought was that they looked exactly the same, except her mother was older, heavier, and appeared worn out. Sarah should have come alone, but she brought her three kids and her husband, who was not Tori's biological father. To the teenage Tori, he seemed like a creep and made her feel uneasy.

Sarah explained she gave Tori up for adoption because she couldn't support her. She wouldn't say much about Tori's dad, not even his name, but she did confirm what Tori's cousin had told her. Her adoptive parents were actually her great aunt and uncle. Sarah had been phoning them for years, asking for permission to see her, and they had refused. The reunion lasted only thirty minutes, but before departing they worked out a plan to call and write to each other without Tori's parents knowing. When the good-byes were spoken, surprisingly neither one shed a tear.

Within two months John and Kate found out about the clandestine meeting. Kate cried tears of anger, feeling betrayed by Tori's actions. John's response was the opposite. He was angry with Tori for being sneaky. It was stunning to Tori that neither of them understood why she was so determined to meet her biological mother. Sarah sent letters and occasionally called on the phone, but the promises to stay connected didn't last long. Three years to be exact. She said she loved Tori, but the lack of birthday cards, Christmas gifts, or any other form of contact convinced Tori otherwise. Her biological mother had walked away once again.

Upon graduating from high school, Tori enrolled in college and majored in music. She moved into an apartment with a friend and landed a job as a nurse's aide. Amid chaos and financial strain she moved back and forth from the apartment to her parents' home, all the while searching for a place to belong. A mess financially and emotionally, she moved from relationship to relationship, many of them abusive, sometimes physically and sometimes verbally. These bad relationships seemed to be the only constants in her life, but her whole world was about to change.

A person can never know when he will meet someone who alters the course of his life. Tori was no different. One night a friend recommended that she meet a man who worked with her husband. Tori was not interested, but the friend insisted the two were a perfect match. Behind Tori's back the friend arranged for both of them to be at her house on the same night. By the time Ron arrived, Tori had thrown back enough Crown Royal to be fairly toasted. They visited a while then left and went to Ron's house.

When she woke up the next morning, she barely remembered any details of the night before. Ron drove Tori back to her car and asked for her number. When he called later that night, the conversation lasted for hours. Tori was excited when they started seeing each other every day.

She wanted to settle down, and Ron seemed like a good candidate. Not only did he give good advice, but he also felt like a father figure. Against her parents' wishes, she moved in with him a mere six months after they had met.

Soon after Tori settled in with Ron, his job transferred him to another city, so Tori packed up and went with him. Sixteen months after the blind date, Tori and Ron were married in a small church before a group of about thirty people. The crowd was made up entirely of Ron's friends and family, except for five people who knew Tori: Kate and John, one girlfriend, and her two siblings. Sarah wasn't invited.

Like any other married couple, Tori and Ron had their ups and downs. Sometimes he would threaten to leave, but she couldn't bear the possibility. Meaningless arguments over trivial matters often brought Ron to a quick boil. Usually by the time the argument was over, neither could even remember what it was about. But one night things got out of control when Ron criticized her "disgusting" tacos. The brawl ended with Ron saying he was calling it quits. Tori got down on her knees, grabbed his pants leg, and begged him to stay. They weathered the storm, but rough seas got choppier when Ron lost his job and they were forced to move in with his parents.

After a major blowup about her mother-in-law, Tori moved out. She didn't really want things to end; she just wanted Ron to apologize. More than that she wanted what most every woman wants—a man who was willing to fight for her, especially since her birth mother had given her up. Contrary to Tori's expectation Ron let her go without putting up much of a fight. It was sickening, familiar territory. Within a short year and a half, the divorce papers were wet with ink.

Newly single, Tori moved into a place of her own. She felt lonely and hated the walls that seemed to be closing in. Even though she despised the thought of living with her mom and dad, it was better than facing life alone, so she moved back home.

While she and Ron remained unusually good friends and constantly stayed in touch, Tori began occasionally dating others. Ron wasn't too pleased. He didn't want her, but he didn't want anyone else to have her either. As more days on the calendar were marked off with an X, the pair considered repairing the breach. Ron sent Tori a lengthy love letter that she let Kate read. After Kate heard how Ron felt, she asked why they didn't get back together. When Tori couldn't think of an answer, she knew it was time to try and work things out. Four weeks later Ron and Tori remarried; shortly thereafter Tori became pregnant.

Part of Ron's solution to keep the marriage on track was to get back into church. Both he and Tori had accepted Christ as children, but neither had anyone to help them grow in their faith. They were extremely immature in their beliefs, never having moved beyond their initial commitment. A lukewarm belief was the only kind they had ever known.

They had no idea God wanted to do more than take them to heaven or that knowing Him wasn't just about going to a Sunday morning meeting. Going through the motions and trying to live up to a phony, legalistic check-list brought little satisfaction. When arguments over petty issues led half of the congregation to leave, Tori and Ron decided it was no longer worth the effort and quit going themselves.

For several years the marriage was a roller coaster. At the bottom of one bumpy, stomach-churning hill, Tori gave Ron an ultimatum. They were going to counseling or she was leaving, so Ron agreed to attend the sessions. Two daughters had been born, Ron's greatest joy, and he wasn't going to part with them, no matter what Tori required. Something about them changed Ron into a better, more settled man.

Their relationship withstood the pain and the ugly truths revealed in the counseling sessions. Digging up bones so they could be properly reburied was a messy but necessary business. Ron and Tori understood the importance of keeping the family together. The turbulence didn't end with the counseling sessions, but one thing had changed. Tori and Ron were determined to honor the promise they made before God and stay together until death, no matter what storms came.

Tori worked at several different companies and did well. But something was still missing. One day she saw a newspaper ad about a part-time job as a secretary. She turned in an application and was called in for an interview. As one of several applying, she would be notified within a couple of weeks. She was shopping when the call came telling her someone else had been chosen. Even though this was a Christian company and her experience at church hadn't been great, for some reason this job felt like a good fit, so the news was a big letdown.

The woman selected for the job worked four weeks before her husband asked her to quit. She didn't want to comply, but desiring to submit to her husband, the woman turned in her two-weeks notice. Shortly thereafter Tori received a call from the company telling her they might still be interested.

During the interview Tori realized the two men asking her questions were not just church members but people who had deep, committed relationships with Jesus. Tori thought her spiritual life, though not fulfilling, was as good as it could get. Seeing the lives of the Christians she worked with opened her eyes to possibilities she never knew existed. She began seeking God with a new hunger that grew deeper every day. There was no aha moment or giant leaps of faith. The growth in her heart was slow but steady, and in time it began to affect Ron and the girls.

It's ironic that Tori got the job because a woman submitted to her husband's request. Her whole life Tori thought submission meant giving others a license to throw her under the bus. But when she surrendered to the tug of God on her heart, she found the submission she once feared to be empowering. Instead of expecting rejection, she began to welcome love. She quit making excuses, confronted her pain, and asked God to use her life to bless someone else.

When Tori forgave Sarah for the abandonment, she set them both free, no longer allowing her biological mother's actions to define her. Instead of trying to change Ron, she left that job in God's hands. She had her own issues to confront, issues God was healing step by painful step.

Instead of looking for her identity in her birth parents, friends, husband, or even her children, Tori found her identity in her relationship with God. She never received a sign from heaven or experienced some miracle to prove God really existed and was in charge of her life. But she sees His handiwork in her and her family as day by day she chooses to do things His way.

At one time Tori could have only dreamed that God would change her life, but today she is seeing things come to pass that she has been trusting God to do for years. Tori's relationships with John, Kate, Sarah, and Ron are not where she wants them to be, but through God's grace they are not where they were. In a twist of the divine, the woman who submitted to her husband and quit her job not only became a close friend of Tori's but also now works with her. Four years ago Tori said yes to a future no longer defined by the past, and she has never looked back.

Chapter 12

DRASTIC MEASURES

I MET SAM THROUGH a mutual friend named John. I found him intriguing. A former military man, Sam was strong, stocky, and inked down both arms with tattoos he had gotten in younger, wilder days. He was a good, hardworking man but clearly not someone you wanted to cross. Whether because of his size or his no-nonsense personality, most people found him a little intimidating.

Sam was married to a talkative woman he met while doing a tour of duty overseas. They had two good-looking children and, unbeknownst to me or his closer friends, a marriage and life in turmoil. Sam didn't say much to anyone unless it needed to be said, so I was a fairly surprised when he pulled me aside one night when a group of us met at a local restaurant. Standing with both hands in his pocket and his normal swagger gone, he looked me straight in the eye and casually asked if he could call sometime to talk about some issues he was working through.

"Sure, man! Is everything OK?" I didn't ask because I sensed any alarm; it was an automatic response. Scratching the side of his head he replied, "Yeah, it's all good. I just wondered what your opinion might be on some things."

Because I was curious, I considered for a second prying the lid open. I quickly decided otherwise. Sam was placid about the whole thing, so I figured the issue was probably nothing major. Plus I figured if he wanted to talk right then, he would have done so. After all, Sam wasn't the kind of guy who could be pressed. If only I had known he was gasping for air.

Sam was a very private man, so no one knew his wife's money-squandering ways had driven them to the brink of bankruptcy and divorce. Busy with my own selfish focus, I didn't give him or his question any more thought until the phone rang around 11:00 p.m. less than two weeks later. On the other end of the line was my friend John. As he tried to talk, I could hear someone screaming in the background.

"Jay, I may need your help tonight," he said. "I need to find somewhere for Sam's boys to stay."

"John, I don't mind them staying here, but...can you hear me OK?"

He raised his voice. "Barely. Can you speak a little louder?"

"I was just saying, I don't mind the kids staying here, but they don't know Missy or me and might be a little leery. What the heck is going on? Where are you, man? I can barely hear you because of all the screaming!"

"Hold on while I step outside."

Through the phone I heard a door shut, then John continued. "I am at Sam's. The authorities just left, because..." Hair-raising screams interrupted him, which made me think someone must have followed him out the door. Then I heard John telling Sam's wife, "Everything will be alright, and the kids will be fine. Go back in the house for a couple of seconds, and I'll be right back in."

John then turned his attention back to me. "Jay, I've got awful news. Sam committed suicide, and his wife is going insane. She found him in the house, but the kids didn't see anything. Pray for the family as they walk through this terrible tragedy. If I need you and Missy, I'll call back. I've got to go!"

I immediately recalled our conversation at the restaurant, and Sam's plea became crystal clear. It made sense now, but why didn't I pick up on the change in his behavior sooner? Sam wasn't the kind of guy to want to talk about his problems with anyone, let alone another man. How could I be so clueless? I wondered why I didn't take his question more seriously. I felt guilty and nauseous for unintentionally neglecting him. I sat on the sofa wondering if a call would have prevented his death. Sometimes the warning signals from a suicidal person can be so hard to discern.

I was honored by the invitation to serve as a pallbearer at the funeral. It was excruciating. Sam's wife was a justifiable wreck. She kept screaming Sam's name and practically had to be carried out when the service ended. Never before or since have I witnessed such emotion at a funeral. The service ended quickly, but I knew for those left behind the pain would never really end.

I left the funeral that day thinking about Sam and what

the last few moments of his life must have been like. I found myself asking why he made such a selfish decision to give up, but I only thought about this briefly because I already knew the answer.

My earliest childhood memories are from a time when my family lived in San Antonio, Texas. Dad was a successful insurance salesman, and my mom stayed at home raising my sisters and me. We lived a middle-class lifestyle in a nice two-story house. I had a good buddy named David, who lived down the street. We did stupid stuff like catching snakes and lighting plastic cups of gasoline on fire. One day I tried to scare Mom in her bedroom by taking a garter snake we found and pulling it from behind my back. It was funny until she freaked out, knocked it out of my hand, and called my dad. When he got home, I paid the consequences.

Life was good, especially the summer Dad built us a huge tree house that was as good as any professional architect could design. When it was complete, we were determined to spend the night inside it—that is, until the mosquitoes gnawed on us with the vengeance of a vampire. There was nothing particularly unique about my childhood. I played sports as a kid. I chased the family dog, which was always a large breed such as a German shepherd or Irish setter. And as the middle child and only boy, I fought constantly with my two sisters.

Our parents were deeply committed to their faith. Mom read her Bible so often the pages looked like they were from ancient scrolls. And she prayed constantly, even for small things like a good parking spot at the shopping center when none was available. Every morning before school Mom read the Bible aloud and prayed for us while we ate breakfast. Church and conversations about God were part of our everyday life, and our weekly routine included spending Sunday mornings at Castle Hills Church. I naïvely thought everyone lived the same way we did.

Mom accepted Christ as a young girl, but my dad was never interested in spiritual matters until after he met my mom. He became a Christian a couple of years after they married. Due to the change their faith brought into their lives, they told me about Jesus and my need to become a Christian from the time I was a child. When I was somewhere around second grade, I repeated a prayer with them in the hallway of our home, asking Jesus to forgive me of my sins and to come into my life. Mom said as a new Christian I should make my decision public and be baptized as soon as possible. The following Sunday we walked the aisle of our church together so I could tell the preacher what happened to me earlier in the week. That night Mom and Dad, full of pride, watched me go under the water.

From then on my beliefs were primarily based on what I heard from my parents. When my sisters and I were growing up, our mom did most of the teaching about God while our dad spent much of his time working. Their faith was tested on many occasions, but they continually held their ground. One of those instances occurred when we went to see a two-story house that was under construction. I was playing chase upstairs with my older sister when I ran over a mat covering a hole in the floor. I landed headfirst on the bottom steps.

Unconscious, I was rushed to the hospital. When the x-rays came back, the doctor told my parents I had sustained permanent brain damage. He said I might be in a vegetative state the rest of my life. My parents called the preacher to have him and the church pray. Mom told the doctor she wouldn't accept his professional diagnosis because she believed God would heal me. Hours later I awoke for the first time since the fall with Mom lying across my legs in prayer. I clearly remember being totally coherent and asking why I was in the hospital. After running the same scans again, the doctor cleared me to go home and gave me a clean bill of health. It was as though I'd never even fallen.

Mom believed God miraculously healed me, and so did the doctor despite his claim to not be a Christian. Although Mom regularly reminded me of the miracle, for years afterward I often lay in bed wondering if God was real. My doubts grew as I entered junior high. On one occasion I told my mom about a friend at school who was asking me how he could be sure he was going to heaven. In truth, I was actually the "friend" with the doubt.

One night when I was twelve years old, I foolishly tested God. I told Him if He was real, then He should prove it the next day by allowing me to break my leg. At recess the very next morning I was playing dodge ball and fell on my knee. Mom immediately picked me up from school and took me to the doctor for x-rays. My knee was cracked and engorged with a hematoma the size of a tennis ball. I was fitted with a cast, which I liked because it got me more attention from girls and fewer chores, but I didn't find the proof of God's existence I was seeking.

Like many who test God, I wasn't completely convinced. I thought the accident might have been a coincidence.

By the time I entered my freshman year of high school, I had no desire for any part of church even though my parents required it. Like many people who grew up around spiritual influences, I took my Christian heritage for granted and became thoroughly unresponsive. To me church was nothing more than a social club. I never felt connected or like going made any lasting difference in my life.

During my sophomore year peer pressure hit a boiling point. I started dating a beautiful blonde whose father was an alcoholic. After a short time I wanted to break up, but she threatened she would do "something crazy" and began crying. When I got home that night, her friend called from the hospital to say she had attempted suicide by overdosing on pills. I went to see her, arriving shortly after they pumped her stomach. It was the last time I saw her, but she left a lasting impression. She became the first person I ever knew who attempted to end her life. Later that week her parents sent her to a girls' home out of state.

Mom and dad were strict but not over-the-top. Boundaries were defined and enforced. There were no double standards; we were not asked to avoid anything they weren't avoiding themselves. My parents didn't drink, and as long as we lived under their roof, they made it clear their kids wouldn't do so either. Mom always told me to be careful who I spent time with because my friends were a picture of my future. Somehow it didn't register until it was too late.

Two of my friends from the football team introduced me to alcohol one night. I didn't like the taste, but I did like the buzz it gave me and the acceptance of my friends. I quickly learned how to conceal my actions from my folks. On most weekends and often during lunch breaks at school my buddies and I would sneak off to drink. None of my friends at church were any different from me. Most of them drank alcohol and for one purpose—to get wasted! On Sundays we went to church and laughed about how smashed we got the night before.

Not only did I get heavily mixed up in the party scene during my high school days, but I also became promiscuous. My parents discouraged sex before marriage, but I didn't share the same convictions. The perception was that the guys were normally the aggressors, but my experience proved otherwise. Many times the girls made the first moves, and "church" girls often were some of the most aggressive, especially if they were in a semi-committed relationship.

My promiscuity became a vicious cycle. Every month I would promise myself that if my girlfriend didn't get pregnant, I would stop the madness. My promises were never kept. I spent a large portion of my high school years in fear. My behavior not only kept me from enjoying some of life's most special years, but it also created some emotional webs that were not easily untangled. I sporadically felt guilty but possessed neither the desire nor willpower to stop.

After graduation I went off to college in Abilene, Texas. My parents steered me toward Christian schools, which was fine with me since I just wanted to be in a new town living on my own. My college was supposed to be a Christian school, but the environment wasn't much different from the secular universities my friends attended. In my opinion the college was more religious than it was spiritual. We were required to attend chapel every week, but it felt like we were just going through the motions. Like most of the other students, I did homework or slept during chapel instead of listening to the dry speakers.

The school was way too legalistic for me, especially when I found out they didn't want their students to attend the dances at another university across town. That was all the more motivation to visit! We probably wouldn't have considered going if the school hadn't made such a big deal out of it. But since these dances were being singled out, we wanted to know what was so wicked about them. The dance turned out to be nothing risqué, but many of us students continued going just to be rebellious; we didn't like the school imposing what we believed were legalistic rules.

After a while I gave up the religious front altogether since I no longer had to attend church. I didn't think much about God and became more cynical every month. My roommate was studying to be a pastor, but I lost respect for him pretty quickly when he borrowed money from me and refused to pay back the full amount.

Adding fuel to my fire was an incident with the other preacher-in-training across the hall. One night I walked over to borrow some paper from him. His door was open, so I just barged in. He was sitting on his bed staring at a *Playboy* magazine. When I told him in a joking manner that I thought he was going to be a preacher, he replied,

"Just because I'm a preacher doesn't mean I can't read the articles." This just added to my skepticism about God, church, the school, and my upbringing.

Actually, people who called themselves Christians were negatively influencing me the same way I negatively influenced my classmates in high school. My grades were faltering due to partying, spending too much time with my girlfriend, and neglect. By the end of the first semester I was on academic probation and moving back home. I then enrolled at Midwestern State in my hometown, but my stint there lasted as long as my time at the other college: one semester.

Months later I ran into an old buddy named Ralph at the local mall. When we met my senior year of high school, I thought he was cool because he was from California. He had just lost his roommate and was looking for someone to fill the spot. I was ready to move out of my parents' house, and I had a job making minimum wage at a manufacturing company, so I gladly accepted the opportunity. Two weeks later I moved into his half of a run-down duplex even though it had no air conditioner or refrigerator. We used a cooler for our food and beer and stole the ice after hours from a nearby hotel.

I had no furniture of my own, and since Ralph had no spare bed, I slept on the sofa. Looking back, I can't believe I moved in. The place was a dump. I was accustomed to nice things but never gave any thought to what I was giving up. I just wanted to leave the rules and accountability of my parents. The day I arrived I brought nothing but sheets. Dad gave us a window AC unit because it was unbearably hot, and before long Ralph scored a refrigerator.

Ralph and I had several things in common. Neither of us was in college, we both had dead-end jobs and barely made enough money to get by (even though Ralph worked for his dad), and we both drank like fish. Our childhood and family life were significantly different, though. As a young boy Ralph went through a tragic time when his mother committed suicide. He was at home with her when it happened.

After I moved in, we spent nights at a local bar called The Rock. It wasn't a trendy bar where college-aged people mingled, but a place filled with much older men, most of whom were alcoholics. It was a small, dark, smoky, dingy place with no women and only one pool table we hovered over trying to win money playing Three Ball. The jukebox was stocked with all the latest loving-leaving-cheating-drinking country songs and belted out their moans until last call. In hindsight I'm shocked we never killed ourselves or someone else while driving home.

Compounding my muddy life was the loss of my job a few weeks after I moved in with Ralph. I lived on unemployment for months. Not only did I lose the job, but I also lost my girlfriend and car. Without transportation and all my friends in college or working all day, I spun out of control. I felt like a loser. Not knowing how to deal with the loss of the three most important things in my life, I upped the ante on my drinking. Too much time on my hands and nowhere to spend it led me to look for a mental sedative. Facing my failure was more than I could handle.

I never considered that I might have a drinking problem until Ralph came home one day and told me I needed to get help. Stunned by his words, I asked what he could be referring to.

"What am I referring to? Are you serious? When I leave in the morning, you are drinking. When I get home at night, you are doing the same thing. You need to pull it together, man. You're drunk all the time!"

I assured him I had it under control and could stop whenever I wanted to. I went on to explain that I was just going through a tough time and needed a little pick-me-up during the day. Even though I minimized his concern, I thought about his words...a lot. Ralph drank like a fish himself, and I figured he had no right to point fingers at me. Yet his words stung.

The next morning I quit drinking. My decision to get on the wagon lasted only three days because I knew no other way to escape the weight of depression. But I became much more discreet and was careful about what I allowed Ralph to see. I didn't want any more lectures or to expose my weakness.

A couple of weeks later Ralph came home with a Bible. I thought I must have been hallucinating. When I asked where he got it, he said he had gotten "saved."

I immediately tried to shoot him down. "What do you mean you got saved?"

"Just what I said. I gave my life to Jesus!"

"Come on, bro! I've already been through all that religious stuff, and it doesn't make any difference!"

"I tell you what, Jay. You live your life how you want to live it, but from now on I'm going to live for God."

"Whatever, man. I bet it won't last two weeks!"

Ralph didn't want to go to the bar anymore but was spending all his time with his Christian girlfriend. She committed her life to Christ the same night he did. I resented his getting saved because he no longer wanted to party, and the new situation left me even more alone. Adding to my problem and our tension, I was spending so much of my unemployment check on alcohol I couldn't afford to pay rent. Ralph was threatening to kick me out.

One day I awoke at lunchtime with a hangover. Stumbling into the restroom, I turned on the cold water to quench the fire burning in my forehead. After splashing my face several times, I rose up and looked in the mirror. I was so trashed. After staring at a face I barely recognized, I screamed at the reflection several times, "I hate you!" Then I put my fist through the glass and started crying. Without wiping off the blood, I walked back to the sofa where I was sleeping and decided to do what I had been contemplating for months.

Sitting on the couch in my underwear with both elbows on my legs and my hands on my head, I started sobbing. With my shoulders shaking from emotion, I asked myself the familiar questions I had no answers to. What do I have to live for? What other option do I have? Was God even real, and if so, would killing myself condemn me to hell? Did hell really exist, or was I already there?

I knew of no other way to stop the pain. The walls had closed in to the point that I felt imprisoned. Life was dark, senseless, void. I had no compass. I didn't like the real me or the person I pretended to be in public. At parties I was happy since I didn't have to deal with the reality of who I was, but once I got back home, the tormenting voices began whispering in my thoughts, speaking evil words about solving temporary problems with a permanent solution.

Still sitting in my underwear, I reached under the sofa and grabbed my .22-caliber pistol. I loaded all nine chambers. Partly as a stall tactic, I wanted to solve two riddles bothering me. The first was, If God is real will I go to heaven? The second was, Is the gun strong enough to kill me? I didn't want to just end up brain-dead.

My thoughts drifted back to San Antonio, to the prayer I uttered in the hall with my parents and the simple baptism at church. I concluded that I would definitely go to heaven if God weren't a fable. And I reasoned the gun would do the job if placed it in the right spot. I pulled back the hammer and poked the barrel to my temple.

My hand trembled, and the gun was ticking against my head. I heard a voice in my mind telling me, "Just do it. Hurry and get it over with!" I screamed, closed my eyes, and began to slowly squeeze the trigger.

All of a sudden I thought I heard someone pulling up on our gravel driveway, so I eased off the trigger to see. When the sound continued, I sat the gun down and peeked through the blinds. The green Nissan 240SX told me exactly who it was, but I couldn't figure out what he was doing at the house. I wiped my tears, slid the gun back under the sofa, and turned on the TV so he wouldn't suspect anything unusual. When Ralph unlocked the door and walked in, I didn't look his way.

"What are you doing home?"

Sensing something was up, he replied in a strange tone, "What in the heck is going on?"

"Nothing. Why are you home?"

"You won't believe it. Dad has never done this before, but he walked up to me today and told me to take the rest of the day off with pay."

I wondered if this was a coincidence or God's way of keeping me from killing myself. So I asked, "Why would he do that?"

"I don't know," he said. "I'm just glad to be off."

I didn't consider suicide again for weeks because I thought God had rescued me. I knew Ralph's dad and how unlikely it was for him to pay Ralph for not working. Plus, the timing was too perfect. If Ralph had showed up one minute later, I would have been dead. It was too precise to be luck. And my doubts about God were beginning to diminish because of what was happening in Ralph's life. I no longer knew who he was. He quit drinking, raising hell, and going to clubs, and was studying his Bible every night. I couldn't understand it. He was never the religious type. He didn't grow up in church and certainly had never been a Bible reader.

I noticed he was completing an interactive workbook called *The Survival Kit for New Believers*. At night when I heard him pull up in the driveway, I would turn off the TV and pretend to be asleep to see if he was going to sit at the kitchen table to fill out his book. Once he went to bed, I would sneak the book off the table, get out my flashlight, and get under my covers so I could secretly read the things he wrote. It became the most exciting, and only, thing I had to look forward to.

His words were astonishing. He was writing out prayers, telling God he loved Him, and answering questions in the book with words I couldn't imagine anyone saying to God. Except Mom! It was almost like a love letter written to a girl. I thought Ralph wouldn't last, but he never slowed down, and his authenticity was giving me hope. I saw that he was happy and in some strange way complete. I wanted the peace I could feel absorbing his life. Peace was something I didn't know.

One night I stopped by my parents' house to wash clothes when I heard my name echoing down the hallway. I walked in the den, and Mom was pointing toward the TV. It was a commercial about an upcoming event at her church, and it flashed a clip of a tall, thin guy who looked somewhat like me. I missed most of what was said except the part where he mentioned attempting suicide. Mom asked me to come hear him, but I heartily rejected the offer. I told no one about my suicidal thoughts, but I wondered if somehow Mom knew. I asked her why she wanted me to see the commercial, but when she responded by saying she thought I would like him, I knew my secret was intact.

Every time she mentioned the church event over the next few weeks, I found a way to politely evade the question. Honestly, I had no intention of going. Two weeks rolled by, and it was time for the big event. Mom told me how amazing the first service had been and pleaded with me to come on Sunday night. She was fired up as she told me how dozens of people went forward to accept Christ.

I would never have admitted it, but on more than one occasion I did think about the commercial and considered going. The guy was very dynamic and was the only person I knew of with whom I could relate. When Mom talked about the people who found new hope earlier that morning, I wondered if that could happen to me. As she talked, I felt a pull to go and check it out, but the feeling didn't last long. Later that day a friend called and asked me to go drinking. I agreed, deciding I would rather chill with friends than hear some spiel about Jesus.

Strangely, my friend never showed. When it became clear he was standing me up, I looked at my watch and realized the service was just about to start. I debated with myself whether I should go and decided to drive by and just see what was going on. Once I got there, I couldn't leave. I sat in the parking lot for twenty minutes drinking Silver Bullets and listening to Guns and Roses because I knew the routine and didn't want to hear the old school hymns. I planned to wait until that part was over, sneak into the balcony so no one would see me, and then leave the second the speaker was finished.

I put my plan in motion, but I was startled as I crept up the back stairs into the balcony. I figured few people would be attending, but it was almost completely packed. My timing was perfect, though. As soon as I sat down the evangelist walked to the platform. His words were not loud, but they were piercing. I didn't like listening to preachers, but he was different. No peculiar hair, strange demeanor, or churchy words. He was the first preacher I ever thought seemed cool. He was young, passionate, and real. I was captivated by his words, which hit me like bullets from a machine gun. I sincerely wondered if someone told him about me because he was saying so many things that related to my life.

Halfway into his sermon the preacher began talking about the crucifixion of Christ. I had heard the story hundreds of times, but I had never heard it told this way. I knew he believed every word as he graphically explained every detail. He told how Jesus was stripped naked, tied to a pole, hit with a cat-o'-nine-tails thirty-nine times, and then had a crown of three-inch thorns pummeled onto his head. He intentionally noted that each leather strip on the cat-o'-nine-tails had a piece of bone or metal attached to the end so it would dig out chunks of flesh.

When he got to the cross, he said spikes were driven into Jesus's feet and hands so He could be hoisted in the air like a scarecrow. With broken ribs, a shredded back, and asphyxiation setting in, Jesus pushed up and down, with His tortured feet pressing against the jagged cross, to gasp for air. Just about everyone hurled insults at Him, including the religious leaders. I was so caught up in the story I forgot I wasn't actually there.

What bothered me most was when he told of how God turned His back on His Son because of my sin. He said Jesus asked God to forgive the people who were crucifying Him because they didn't understand what they were doing. But why would He request this? It didn't make sense to want the people who murdered you to be set free.

As my thoughts swirled, I felt anger toward the Roman soldiers who brutally mocked Him. Then I heard the preacher say, "You are responsible for His death. You're no different than the soldier who pounded the nails into His hands. Many of you have mocked Him with your life, but He loves you anyway, just like He did the soldiers. The purpose of His death was to give you a life. You cannot be good enough. You can't earn forgiveness."

When he said Jesus came to give "life," I remembered my suicide attempt and wondered if I could have a life instead of just an existence. He closed the talk by saying, "Some of you may never have another opportunity to accept Christ as your Savior. Maybe you thought you were a Christian but now realize you never turned from your sin to put your faith in Jesus. If you say no tonight, your heart could become hardened until you one day find yourself eternally separated from God."

Conviction held my mind and heart in a vise. Although I had often thought I was a Christian who had drifted away, the truth was inescapable. I didn't know Jesus personally; I just knew about Him. Tears fell from the corners of my eyes. I felt such guilt for my sinful ways and my unwillingness to give God the glory and allegiance He deserved. I had not only rebelled against God, but I had also robbed Him. I was starving to have Jesus in my life. I couldn't remember wanting anything as desperately as I wanted Him that night. I didn't care if it cost me my friends, parties, vices, or everything else. Jesus traded His life for mine, and now I was ready to trade my life for His.

The evangelist asked people to come forward to pray for salvation and publicly acknowledge their commitment to Jesus. I wondered if anyone felt like me. I wondered if anyone would come forward. I looked down and saw a guy named Barry walking down the aisle, wiping his eyes. We used to play street basketball together, and I never liked him or his crazy-eyed brother-in-law. We argued continually about fouls, and they were always slamming beers between games. Even though he was no worse than me, I judged him as worse. Seeing him go forward did something to me. I figured if he could be forgiven, then so could I.

Within minutes dozens of people were standing together at the front. I dropped to my knees, no longer concerned with what others might say or think and began asking Jesus to forgive me and be my Savior. I wasn't repeating words as I did when I was a child. I genuinely wanted Christ in my life, and my plea came from a deep, sincere place in my heart. When I got up from my knees, the doubt about Jesus was gone. So were the guilt and shame. I didn't hear any voices or see any visions, but I felt a peace I had never known and a certainty that God was in my life. When everyone was dismissed, I walked out the door and immediately noticed the moon. I thought to myself that the world didn't look the same anymore. I got into my truck and threw away all the beers. Driving down the road, I couldn't get over the excitement and the new way I felt inside. I began to weep, because I finally felt fulfillment.

Mom didn't know I went to church, and I didn't want her to know. I did want to see and be near her, though, so I drove home. I decided not say anything about what happened to me in case my life-change didn't last. After all, I wouldn't want to let her down or be held to a standard I might not be able to maintain. Somehow, knowing her God had become my own made me want to be in her presence.

When I arrived home, my parents had some friends over from church, and everyone was sitting in the den talking. I stonewalled my evening's agenda and just listened while they visited. No more than ten minutes after I sat down, Mom asked me, "Son, did you go to church tonight?"

I tried to dodge her question. "Mom, I already told you I wasn't going. Why would you even ask me that?"

She had a suspicious yet gentle look on her face as

she replied. "I thought about you during the service and hoped you might be there. Plus something about you looks different."

I just shrugged my shoulders. I was about to burst. I wanted to tell her, but I kept up the charade. I sat in the den with the four of them for the next hour and listened while they talked about the service. That night I couldn't sleep for thinking about what happened to me. I felt love in a way I never felt it before. It was no longer some abstract concept I tried to give, receive, or feel but something unstoppable, living, and controlling the inside of me.

The next morning I woke up with a desire to start reading the Bible. I never had any interest in reading it before, except on rare occasions when I got into some big trouble and needed a bailout. The scriptures never made sense to me. Now all of a sudden the words leaped off the pages. I couldn't get enough. It wasn't something I was doing out of duty, but something my new heart longed for. I began memorizing verses. It took three days to memorize my first. Within months I would be memorizing three a day, and less than twelve months after accepting Christ I could quote several hundred.

Days after meeting Christ, I told my mom about being at the service and informed her I had become a Christian. She told me I was mistaken, that I was already a believer and reminded me of the day I prayed with her in the hallway. I told her I didn't understand the prayer, had no concept of genuine faith, and my belief had never been anything more than an intellectual assent. Initially she couldn't accept that all those years my faith was not real. A week later she came up to me and said, "Jay, I was wrong. You really did get saved for the first time."

When I asked how she came to this conclusion, she gave me a puzzled look and said, "I don't even know who you are anymore. You are a completely different person than you have ever been. I see something in you only God could have done."

I wasn't aware how quickly I was changing, but hearing her affirming words made me feel proud.

I knew for sure the change God brought in my life was permanent when I hooked up with some buddies a week later. We started drinking, and I went too far. When I woke up the next morning, I was overcome with conviction. I was not accustomed to feeling regret over getting drunk. It never bothered me before, but I felt devastated for letting God down. It dawned on me that my heart and mind now felt what I could never make it feel on my own. What I could never change from the outside, God was changing from the inside. I went to all my buddies and told them I had given my life to Christ. They weren't impressed, but I was unashamed and unapologetic about who Jesus was and what He was doing in my life.

I was so burdened for my friends I begged God to use me to help them find Christ. I never strong-armed my buddies, but I did vow to tell each one of them how they could know Jesus. One friend in particular was really strung out, so I went to his house to tell him about the peace I had found. He told me he appreciated my caring but was not ready to live for God because it would cost him too much.

This response was repeated on numerous occasions. I remained unfazed. I knew they were looking to see if my commitment would last. They weren't negative but didn't understand why I wouldn't participate in some of our old ways, especially drinking. Most of them were able to keep their alcohol consumption in check, but since I was unable to do so, I quit altogether. I ended up losing almost every friend.

Losing those relationships was one of the most difficult realities of my new life with Christ. I missed being invited to hunts, the lake, and parties. I could tell my old friends weren't comfortable around me anymore, not because I was always preaching to them but because we were focused on different things. I didn't want to discuss who was getting wasted, throwing a bash, or scoring with the girls; they didn't want to talk about Jesus.

I always worked toward keeping the doors open with my old buddies, going out of my way to stay in touch. In the years since then many of them have become believers, and several of the ones who have not become Christians contact me occasionally for advice or prayer when life gets hard. For every relationship God removed, He replaced it with a better one. I'm still changing but often surprised by the wrong things I'm capable of doing.

To this day I've never gotten over what Christ did for me on the cross or the inexplicable love He has continually piled on me. Years later my relationship with Him is still so fresh. It is delightfully ridiculous that God wanted someone as wicked as me to be a part of His family and that He was willing to use such drastic measures to make it possible.

Chapter 13

BEHIND CLOSED DOORS

AT SIX FEET four and 270 pounds, Kyle is a picture of strength. He is twenty-two years old and wears his hair short and spiked in the front. Confident yet humble, Kyle grew up in the glamorous city of Dallas and was raised by his mother, Barbara, in a single-parent home. To neighbors, Kyle and Barbara seemed fairly normal. He was a good kid; she was a single mom trying to do her best. But neighbors rarely know what happens behind closed doors.

Kyle adored his mother, and the feeling was mutual. Barbara doted over Kyle, constantly showering him with affection. They were relatively poor, but Kyle's mom never let her son go hungry or do without. She couldn't always give him the latest name-brand shoes, clothes, or electronic device, but he had what he needed.

Barbara worked out of her apartment trying to make a little extra money by cutting her friends' hair. A cleft palate at birth led to numerous surgeries that left her with incessant migraine headaches. The pounding in her head was so severe it became debilitating. Unable to hold a steady job, she became dependent on government disability checks—and pain medication.

Kyle never gave her hankering for pills any thought. Like any other child, he assumed everybody's mom was like his own. He thought nothing of the times they traveled into Mexico so Barbara could get more "medicine." As he grew older, he began to piece together why she was always going to different doctors. Getting numerous physicians to prescribe the same painkillers allowed her not only to stay medicated but also to sell the leftovers.

Besides her ability with scissors Barbara had one other means of earning money. Attractive with deep blue eyes and sandy blonde hair, she stood at six feet two and was frequently complimented on her long, shapely legs. For a short season she sold herself out to the highest bidder, something Kyle didn't know until he was a teenager.

Kyle did grow up seeing boyfriends shuffle in and out of the house and Barbara's life like it was nothing more than a turnstile. The men she gave herself to were better at paying bills than being husbands or fathers. It wasn't officially prostitution, but it worked the same way. As long as she made herself available, they would contribute some money to pay the bills that were stacking up.

Barbara earned a reputation for being easy, though she was just trying to keep food in Kyle's stomach and pills in her own. There were better options for earning a living, but she could see none of them at the time. The way Barbara brought Kyle up was a mirror reflection of her own life as a child. Her mom had been married four times, leaving Barbara with a disengaged, unstable father figure herself. She was accustomed to men never hanging around.

There was one man who stayed connected to Kyle and Barbara. His name was Matthew. A musician and regular drug user, Matt would visit for a few months then leave for several more. Kyle loved him dearly and thought he was the greatest man on earth. Barbara appeared to love him as well, at least when Kyle was around.

Barbara had been with so many men she wasn't sure who Kyle's father was. She'd had several former boyfriends take paternity tests, but none of the men tested positive, including Matthew. Everyone thought the clinic must have made a mistake processing the DNA test because Kyle looked so much like Matt. When pictures of Kyle and Matt were placed side by side, anyone could see the similarity.

For reasons Kyle could not fully explain, Matt was the one he called Dad, and the two had a special bond. That's why the pain hit so hard when he learned Matt died from a heroin overdose when he was eight. What made it worse was that Kyle didn't find out until he was eleven. For three long years he waited and waited, thinking his father would be coming home someday. Kyle never knew why his mother waited so long to tell him. Whenever he asked, Barbara skirted around his questions, attempting to avoid the real issue.

Barbara had never been one for attending church, but one day a bus came through the neighborhood, and a driver was handing out snacks to kids as they got on. When Kyle asked the man how he could get a snack, the driver said he gave them to all the kids who went to church. That was all the motivation he needed to get on the bus the next Sunday. Barbara didn't mind him going, and Kyle actually made new friends and enjoyed the services. He would ask her to attend, but she would go only on Easter or Christmas. When she did tag along, she made fun of the people, calling them "religious freaks."

During the summers Kyle went to church camp and became good friends with the youth minister. Eventually he started playing drums there. At one point he even told the preacher he wanted to become a Christian. From that day forward there were many times in his life when he sensed an inner desire to get involved in some kind of ministry.

Much like a wide-awake dream, he could imagine himself standing in front of groups of people, leading them and helping them. No matter how much he wrestled with the possibility, it felt so impossible. What could God do with someone like him, someone with so little to offer? Kyle couldn't have known that his weaknesses made him a prime candidate for God, just the type who would ensure that God received the credit if He did anything great through him.

Kyle didn't know until he was thirteen that for years Barbara had been taking more than pain medication. The day he found her smoking marijuana, there was a confrontation. She explained that she smoked weed to cope with the migraines, and she promised to never use again. It was the only time he ever caught her, but he knew she never stopped. Both sides just pretended nothing was going on until a few months later when Barbara's behavior became very strange during a weekend getaway to celebrate New Year's Eve.

On the trip out of town with some friends she began doing weird things: flipping people off, stealing from the hotel, and acting like she was possessed. When they finally returned home, she started locking herself in the bathroom for hours. Two days later Kyle became so fearful for her, he decided to pick the lock on the door. He rushed in to see his mother with her arm outstretched and a needle buried in her vein. Shooting up brought a rush of heroin that was soon followed by anger.

For the first time in Kyle's life Barbara began to beat him. When she finally let up, Kyle ran to call his grandmother. When Barbara saw what he was doing, she struck him repeatedly with the phone and told him to never tell her mom what he saw. He was close to her mother, and Barbara worried that she might call the authorities or take him away. For the next few days she made Kyle stay in his room and kept his door locked. She covered the television and every window in his room with towels. For unknown reasons she even turned off the breaker so there would be no electricity in his room. Drug-induced paranoia was making her insane.

Kyle managed to break away when his mom failed to lock the door, and he snuck out to the apartment of a woman who lived nearby and attended the church. He told her about his mom, and she called the police. Once the men in blue arrived, Barbara denied Kyle's allegations. She blamed her medication and her disobedient son for the strange scene at the house. The police told Kyle they would put him in juvenile detention if he didn't return home. When the officers left, Kyle begged his mother to stop using, but she told him it was impossible for her to quit.

A few hours later at 3:00 a.m., the police barged through the front door with guns drawn. Barbara had called 911 to say someone was trying to kill her son. Kyle explained to the police that his mom was a drug user who was tripping out and not thinking clearly. Barbara convinced the cops she accidentally took too many pills to soothe her relentless migraines. Once again she was able to conceal the truth.

Before going to his room, Kyle spoke the most cutting words he had ever uttered to his mother: "Mom, I hate you." The words were not from his heart because Kyle worshiped his mother. They were spoken in anger, out of frustration, and in fear of not knowing what was happening to the most important person in his life.

The next day Kyle awoke at 9:00 a.m., walked past his mother's room, and saw her curled up on the bed. After going back to his room, he drifted off to sleep and woke up again two hours later. Groggily stepping through the hallway, he went to check on his mom and saw her lying in the same position she was in earlier.

Immediately he knew something was very wrong because her pounding headaches normally made her twist and turn in her sleep. Kyle ran into his mom's room and grabbed her arm. It was unnaturally cold. He shook her upper torso like a rag doll, and when he released her, she fell back on the bed completely limp. In that moment Kyle knew his mother was gone. It was just a week after New Year's Day.

Kyle's hair-raising screams and calls to 911 didn't alter the outcome. His mother was dead. The coroner's report revealed that she clearly died of a drug overdose. Kyle had no idea then how common addiction was among his mother's family members. His uncle would drink himself to death less than twelve months later.

In preparing for the memorial service, Kyle dug out an old picture of his mom to display at the funeral home. Because he didn't have a frame, he took one off the wall of their apartment. When he removed the backing, he found two pornographic pictures of his mother and a man he didn't recognize. The pictures and the information he slowly gleaned from friends and family revealed Barbara had been involved in the sex industry. For Kyle the news was heartbreaking. It was an awful time to learn more of his mom's secrets. But that wasn't the worst of it.

The pictures left their own scars. He couldn't seem to erase the images from his memory, not only because they were of his mom but also because they triggered something in him he didn't know how to shut off. Before long he was struggling with an addiction to pornography, creating false ideas and fantasies about women, love, and intimacy.

With nowhere else to go Kyle moved in with the one family member with whom he had always been close, his grandmother. He had been spending time with her regularly since the day he was born. In Kyle's mind nothing could ever put a wall between them. But from the day Barbara died, his grandmother began asking him why he didn't tell her what was going on.

Although she didn't initially blame Kyle, he felt she was holding him responsible. Eventually her feelings came to light, and she made it clear that if he had acted differently,

Barbara would still be alive. The pain of losing his mom cut deep enough, but the loss of his relationship with his grandmother only deepened the wound.

Kyle was thirteen years old when his mother died. Lots of young men grow up without their fathers, but few have to grow up without mom. Boys need their mothers. A mother's love is like magic; it transcends time, circumstance, and mistakes. Good mothers don't stop loving their children if that love is not returned. They give without expecting anything in return.

No one else can do what a mother does or be who she is to her child. Before her child is born, a mother is acutely acquainted with the baby's ways. I witnessed this truth in action when my toddler drifted away in a crowded shopping center during the holiday season. My wife thought he was with me, and I thought he was with her. When the error became evident, she was able to detect his faint voice despite the roar of the crowd. It was a remarkable and impossible feat that left me again in awe of moms.

A mother knows her children better than almost anyone else, even when they are grown. When everyone else walks away, mom is often the one willing to stay. On television today I saw a news story about a man who brutally raped and murdered a teenage girl. A mountain of evidence proved without any reasonable doubt that he was the killer. At the sentencing hearing the defense could find only one person to vouch for the man's character. The witness who spoke for the man and begged the judge not to sentence him to death was none other than his own faithful mother.

No one on earth is more committed to her child than a mom. Of course, there are exceptions, women who despise their own flesh and blood and leave deep emotional scars, but more often mothers are a symbol of allegiance and safety. Even in the animal kingdom mothers don't desert their young. When a mother disappears or dies prematurely, the void is like no other and the grief lingers, taking on new forms over time but never going away. So it was with Kyle.

No one knew whether Barbara's death was an accidental overdose or a suicide. Either way Kyle was left without the person who was most important to him. His inability to cope with the loss led him into trouble with the law and a dependence on substances much like the ones that destroyed his mom. He lived with his bitter grandmother until he turned seventeen, but their relationship deteriorated so much that in time she didn't even want him to come home for Christmas.

I met Kyle on the bank of a lake when he was nineteen. He was with his girlfriend, and we talked for about thirty minutes. Through most of our conversation, Kyle wanted to debate the reality of God. He was rather cocky then, wanting to argue anytime I made reference to his need of Christ. To him, surrendering his life to God seemed like an unrealistic solution for someone with so many issues.

At this time he was working at a bank. He had received several promotions, which allowed him to get a small place and move his girlfriend in. Like many other young men, Kyle thought he could find happiness in money, women, and pleasure. He was especially proud of the new truck he was able to purchase, and he loved his new-found independence. "I don't need anybody," he told me.

The drugs he promised himself he would never take were now part of his daily routine. He couldn't see the strongholds destroying his life and taking him down a road that would lead him to the same destination as Barbara. He needed someone to intervene, and the person who stepped in was one Kyle never expected.

One day Kyle met a youth minister who invited him to summer camp. Even though he was older than the students attending, Kyle remembered youth camp as being fun and was eager to take his girlfriend to get away from their routine.

The third night of camp as he listened to the speaker, Kyle felt broken, tired, and sorry for not following Christ. He knew he had once talked with a preacher about becoming a Christian, but that night he knew his commitment to Jesus had never been real. When Kyle returned to his cabin a couple of hours later, his heart was ablaze.

Twenty-four hours later, completely excited, he arrived early to the evening session to grab a seat near the front. Sometime during the talk the speaker walked across the stage and stood right in front of where he was sitting. At that precise moment he felt God was calling him to spend the rest of his life showing others how to find the peace with God he had found. He wanted to live his life for a higher purpose. He wanted—needed—to use his tragic experiences to help others, especially those who had also lost a parent.

The visions he had as a boy were beginning to make sense. People react to tragedy in different ways. Some dive into self-destructive habits. Others live in a prison of guilt or shame. The best and most healing response to life's difficulties is to teach others the lessons learned.

When camp ended, Kyle's life was just beginning. He cut ties with his drug-abusing friends, broke up with his girlfriend, and went off to a school of ministry. He now serves as an associate pastor, youth leader, and church builder. He is constantly amazed at the number of teens he meets who have lost a parent, teens he never would have been able to relate to if he had not lost his own mother, teens God has used him to rescue from self-destructing.

For this reason Kyle says he considers himself fortunate to have gone through such heartbreak. He still misses his mother terribly. And he still feels inadequate to be used of God. But in his sorrow God has given him strength to rescue others drowning in their own. He believes this is why God allowed him to experience the pain in the first place. It is a likely reason God ever allows anyone to encounter pain.

Chapter 14

THE EDGE OF CRAZY

BY ANYONE'S STANDARDS Hunter's prayer was outrageous. Throughout history men in desperate situations have uttered outlandish pleas for God's intervention. This is nothing new or extraordinary, but Hunter's petition was over the edge.

According to most, including his father, Hunter's prayer was inexcusable. He was only eighteen, and this wasn't the kind of request you'd expect from a teenage boy. They don't normally embrace this level of sacrifice. What the naysayers didn't realize was how desperate Hunter had become after asking God for years to make this problem right.

No matter how much he prayed or how deeply he trusted God to answer, he saw no change. So he reasoned it was time to up the ante. By the time he told his father, James, about the deal he'd made with God, Hunter could not be swayed; he would not take his petition off the table. Hunter's simple, heartfelt prayer was difficult for anyone to hear, but for James it was the tipping point.

James grew up in a tight-knit family, the oldest of two children. Because of his mother's job as an apartment manager, James lived in one apartment complex after another. This wasn't as bad as it might seem. James was always meeting new and interesting people. In fact, his childhood struggles did not stem from the places where they lived but rather from within his family's own four walls.

James's mom was obsessive about James and his sister making perfect grades. They were an extension of her, she reasoned, and she couldn't bear for her image to be tarnished. Her perfectionism, like many others', was basically a means of having things done her way. But as far as James knew, he simply could never please her no matter how hard he tried.

His mother had hang-ups for sure, some possibly tied to her childhood years when her father committed suicide. But she was a good mother, a faithful wife, and a committed Christian who, despite her flaws, adored both of her children.

James's father was just as committed to his family. When James was growing up, his dad worked hard at being a plumber, a machinist, and a nonconformist. He was a good husband, father, and provider, and James wanted to be just like him, even with his quirks.

James's dad wore his hair longer than most men did and sported a big gold hoop earring, which was quite unpopular for the times. He liked cigarettes, tattoos, and beer, especially Coors, which was also known as Colorado

Kool-Aid. His priorities turned upside down, however, when the family visited a Christian retreat in Arkansas and he accepted Christ. By the time they arrived home, James's dad had lost his taste for many of the things he previously enjoyed.

Even though their parents were Christians, James and his sister stayed with their grandmother every Saturday night so they could go to church with her on Sunday mornings. Except for the legalism James enjoyed church, but that changed when he became a teenager.

James made good grades, but his mother's pressure at home planted seeds of rebellion that sprouted at school. James made As in his schoolwork but Fs in conduct. His behavior kept him grounded almost the entire school year from friends, television, and hanging out, but that didn't cure him of his rebellious and defiant tendencies. Because of his poor conduct, James ended up spending fifth and sixth grade in a private school.

During those two years James found a way to harness his anger. When it was time for him to begin junior high, he returned to public school and remained there through high school. James was no standout in football or track, but his tall frame, blond hair, and striking blue eyes kept him from being invisible. Despite his good looks, James's first two years of high school were uneventful. Then at sixteen, during his junior year, he tasted some "firsts" that sent him down some thorny paths.

Scoring a job enabled him to buy an eight-year-old blue Chevrolet Camaro. More than making James feel cool, the car gave him the independence he craved. Until then he'd never had a chance to roam with the rowdy crowd; in fact, he spent most of his time by himself. Tired of being in the background, he decided one particularly boring Friday night to no longer be left out of the mix. He blazed from party to party. This is when he scored his first beer, cigarette, and marijuana high, and three minor in possession citations.

His hookup for alcohol was a convenience store where the attractive clerk would sell minors beer even though she knew they had fake IDs. When police cited her for selling beer to minors, James felt genuinely sorry and apologized for getting her in trouble. As a result of his sincere apology, the two swapped phone numbers, and one week later they ended up in the backseat of a car. When deeds were done, she sat and cried, and James felt guilty. For some testosterone tigers, she would have been nothing more than a conquest, a notch on a belt, but not to James. Remorse soaked him. Something he thought would bring him so much pleasure was nothing short of a nightmare. They never spoke again.

By his senior year James was popular in high school. He played in the orchestra, joined the Key Club, was nominated for student awards, and even served as an officer for Students Against Drunk Driving, better known by its acronym SADD. The sad part was that he served as the leader while spending his weekends driving around wasted.

After graduation he enrolled in his hometown college to major in education and join his favorite fraternity. Home wasn't far away, but he moved into the frat house to get out from under his parents' thumb. During his sophomore year the boys held a keg party at an apartment clubhouse. Sitting in the back of a truck, drinking beer, and talking to friends, he saw a girl he barely knew from junior high come walking up with a friend.

He initially noticed her because she was the only person going to the party without shoes on. Her name was Charlene. She was an eighteen-year-old sorority girl from Alpha Phi with a golden mane and pretty face. She was also engaged. No wedding date had been set, but the relationship was serious enough for her boyfriend to offer her a ring. Since her fiancé was out celebrating his twenty-first birthday with his father, Charlene opted to go with some girlfriends to the frat party.

Truth be told, Charlene wasn't really in love with her fiancé. The relationship was on the rocks, and at this point she was only staying with him because he was her first. The emotional ties that came with losing her virginity were binding in more ways than she could have imagined. She was told that sex before marriage was wrong, but she gave away her body because she was convinced they would marry. In Charlene's mind if they married, she wouldn't have made quite as big of a mistake.

At the frat party James and Charlene talked briefly, just long enough for him to invite her to the upcoming annual bash at the river bottom and for her to agree to come. Two weeks later, after getting to know each other at the river celebration, Charlene broke off her rotting engagement, and she and James officially became an item.

Six months later she drove to his house to break some heavy news. As he was cooking dinner, she casually said, "I'm pregnant." His reply was silky smooth, to-the-point, and serious as a coma: "I always thought I would marry you."

After swallowing the last bite, James and Charlene loaded up in the car to tell his parents. James's mom was stoked; his dad didn't show much emotion but did tell him sternly, "You are getting married." Five days later James's parents invited Charlene's mom and dad over for dinner. They hoped to create a buffer to offset the angry outburst expected from Charlene's mother, but nothing worked. She strongly discouraged them from getting married. In her opinion there were other options for a pregnant teenage girl. But marriage is what James and Charlene wanted, and the wedding took place six weeks later. Hunter was born seven months after they exchanged I-dos.

James and Charlene claimed to believe in Jesus, but neither showed much evidence of faith. James made a public commitment as a young boy in a Baptist church, and Charlene prayed for salvation as a teen after reading the Bible at a Methodist retreat. A stronger faith may have made the first year of marriage easier, but the two toughed it out without it. Charlene cried almost every night for the first year. James dropped out of college to begin a series of different jobs. A few years later, dissatisfied and lacking adequate pay, James decided to start his own landscaping company.

Starting a new business was exciting. James and Charlene worked continuously, believing dedicated effort would bring great success. Outwardly the business was growing; they were adding employees and increasing revenue. However, accounting proved they were losing money. Down at the bank the loan officer continued lending more cash, which only made a tight financial situation tighter. The pressure made James look for a way to unwind, and he didn't have to search far. In no time he was using one crutch to kick-start the morning and another to relax once he got home. The pills, alcohol, and tobacco temporarily eased the frustration of an unfulfilling life and failing business.

James hired a woman who quickly became Charlene's best friend. She, like James, was wading through an unfulfilling marriage. Oddly enough, Charlene didn't know her friend and husband were dealing with such feelings. Charlene knew their marriage wasn't perfect, but from her viewpoint she and James were doing fine. James told a different story during his private conversations with the female employee. That was the first mistake. The second was letting one thing lead to another, then another, then another. The doors to treachery opened wide.

Charlene had given birth to their third child six weeks before the day James turned her world upside down. She thought their private trip to the mountains was going to be a lovers' getaway away from the kids. But when they arrived at the summit, James's guilt overwhelmed him, and he confessed to cheating on Charlene for two months. Unloading the guilt brought James relief Charlene didn't feel. For her the confession was like a spear through her heart. Her husband and her friend had been betraying her right under her nose.

When the couple returned home, James's mistress was fired. Never considering divorce an option, Charlene found a way to forgive her husband and her friend. James would make many mistakes, but never again was he unfaithful to his wife. James and Charlene made some changes in their relationship. They attended marriage counseling. They sold the business, and Charlene started going back to church.

James hit the road working different plumbing jobs. He traveled constantly, but the money was better than working a nine-to-five. Over the years a lack of accountability and prolific drug use became James's norm, as did the wall between him and Charlene. Neither was contemplating divorce, but they lived two separate lives that collided only briefly when he was at home between jobs.

Charlene reached a breaking point when she found drugs James had left on the bathroom counter one weekend when he was home. Charlene didn't know her husband had sunk so low. She told him to leave for another job or to just go his own way. There were things she would tolerate, but taking illegal drugs at home and endangering the kids was not one of them.

She concluded that she could make it on her own, and when James came home from the next job, she told him so. James wouldn't agree to a divorce, but he did commit to not bring drugs into the house. The only reason they were staying together was because neither could afford a long custody battle over the children, a war Charlene would have won hands down.

Eleven years of marriage had not transformed James into a good father or husband. By no means was he abusive or mean, just uninvolved. He wasted numerous opportunities to spend time with the kids or attend their events because he was too drunk to participate. Even when James was physically present, he was not always "there." Hunter remembers with fondness the day James gave him his first gun, but James has no recollection it ever happened. Like many other special times, James was present in body yet stoned out of his mind.

Charlene started seeing a counselor and finagled James to attend, but after only one visit he'd had a belly full. The counselor, previously an addict herself, immediately saw through James's crooked lies. Knowing he couldn't weave her into his web of deception, he never went back. The guilty always run from light for fear of exposure.

Although Charlene stayed in the marriage, in reality she had completely given up. But something unexpected happened when the family took a rare vacation. Upon the counselor's advice Charlene approached the trip with openness toward repairing what was broken in their marriage. With that outlook she soon began to enjoy James. Seeing how happy the kids were with their father and remembering how good the good times had been, Charlene decided to fight for the marriage despite James's addiction.

James quit using hard drugs when his drug connection dried up, but he still wouldn't let go of his beer and weed. He hated his alcoholism and knew the toll it was taking on his wife, kids, health, and finances. Like a massive python, addiction was squeezing the life out of him. James sometimes went to church with the family, but he didn't pray for help. He'd never kept the promises he'd made to God to quit, so he figured there was no need in making new commitments he knew he couldn't keep. Not so with Charlene. She was growing in her faith and pleaded with God to help James shake the monster that was destroying him.

Their firstborn, Hunter, was a rare teenager. Despite having an absentee and alcoholic father, he gave every part of his life to Christ. He didn't just go to church, read the Bible, and pray; Hunter loved God with every fiber of his being. Pursuing God and doing His will were all that mattered to him. While his buddies were busy chasing girls, Hunter was busy chasing Christ.

Friends at school respected his unwavering dedication; so did a preacher named Matt, whom Hunter often confided in. Matt saw in Hunter a depth uncommon among even the older men he knew who had followed Christ for years. Matt had no doubt God had His hand on Hunter's life in an unusual kind of way.

Hunter loved James even though he was a pitiful drunk, and he often asked Matt to pray for his father. Not once did Hunter allow his dad's failures to breed resentment in him. Nor did he use his dad's neglect or embarrassing actions as an excuse to rebel against authority. Strangest of all he actually respected his dad and was able to find many good qualities in him. For sure there were open wounds, but not once did Matt hear Hunter utter an accusatory remark about James.

One of the gifts Hunter had received from God was the ability to see potential. He could clearly see the spiritual man James would someday become, even though there was no evidence of it yet. He trusted that God would one day transform James into the father, mentor, and leader he knew he could be.

James didn't know the blitz of prayers Hunter was sending his way. Being tracked by two different hunters, one from above and the other under his roof, began to take a toll on James. One Sunday afternoon in late spring, James stopped by Matt's house saying he just wanted to visit. James was half drunk, thinking he was just being spontaneous, but Matt sensed something supernatural might be going on, because James had never dropped by his house for a conversation. Forty-five minutes of mundane talk on the front porch ended when Matt lit the fuse on a bomb.

"James, when are you going to quit trying to find peace in a can? Your wife and kids need you. You are crushing their heart and God's. This is not the way He intended for you to live! Satan is stomping your butt, and God wants to stop it." This was hardly what James expected to hear, but it proved effective.

James was livid. He wasn't accustomed to anybody confronting him, and Matt knew it. James said he had to leave because he needed another beer. Even though Matt didn't allow alcohol on his property, he didn't want to miss out on an opportunity. "If your chain is wound so tight you have to have another beer, go home and grab one from the cooler, and let's finish this discussion. I know you're man enough to handle the truth."

Matt knew James wasn't the kind of man who would back down from a challenge; he was a guy who had to be handled with brutal honesty. James chugged down two more beers. Then another hour of silk and steel words were exchanged before James told Matt if the conversation was going to continue, he would need a six pack to keep his buzz going. Matt would have to meet him at his house in fifteen minutes.

Matt asked his wife to pray for a miracle before rushing out the door. When he pulled into the driveway, Matt saw

James waiting for him on the porch with a cigarette in one hand and a cold one in the other. Seeing the faded paint chipping off the walls of the scarred house, the result of years of neglect, made Matt think of the scars James had inflicted on his family. If you tell yourself anything long enough, you will eventually be convinced it is true. James assumed his actions would have no long-term effect on his kids, but he was wrong, and Matt was willing to make the truth known.

As the conversation progressed, Hunter came home and joined the two on the porch. He didn't say a word; he just listened intently. Amped up on liquid courage, James began to rant and rave, but Matt refused to back down. He told James he was infected with deception—about his drinking, the effect his addiction was having on his family, and his need for God. On fire and bugging out, James called Matt to the side of the house and got in his face. "Who do you think you are, calling me out in front of my son?"

Matt was sure he was about to be clocked in the face, but he plowed on. "I'll tell you who I am. I am someone who cares enough about you to tell you the truth. If I have to take a butt kicking, that's fine, but your world is sinking around you, and you are out of options. You came to me, and even though you don't know it, it was God who provoked you to do so. God wants this day to be the beginning of the end of your past.

"Your primary problem is not the teeth of addiction but your unwillingness to give yourself to Christ. Give your life to Him, and He will pour out the strength to conquer the rest."

Concerned what might happen, Hunter remained

nearby. James stomped back and forth like a bull before a matador before saying, "All right, Matt. Let's settle this down and be reasonable."

Matt wasn't done. "You're breaking God's heart and your son's. If you don't believe me, just ask him!" James just looked at Hunter without asking him to reply. He didn't need to; James already knew the answer in his heart. He'd known it for years.

James slowly walked back to the front of the house with Matt and Hunter following. Matt broke the uneasy silence when he asked if he could pray before returning home. With permission granted, Matt began to pray.

"God, please do whatever is necessary to get James's attention. You know what buttons need pushing, so I'm asking You to push them. Your love and patience with him don't seem to be enough, so touch him where it hurts before the destruction cannot be undone. Family, finances, job, or health are not off limits. No matter what he has to lose, gaining You will make it worth the exchange. In Jesus's name, amen."

James was bewildered. "I can't believe you just prayed that. I don't want you to pray that way. You're painting me in a corner, opening me up to trouble I don't need. Please don't do that anymore."

Matt was unfazed. "I'm sorry, man, but I won't lie. I am going to pray this every day until you turn to Jesus. Nothing else matters. Whatever you lose to gain Christ is a good trade." With nothing left to be said, Matt hugged Hunter, shook James's hand, and walked away. Only God knew the confrontation would give birth to Hunter's unimaginable prayer.

Seven days passed without Hunter telling James about his request to God. Matt already knew; Hunter had told him the day after his confrontation with James. Not knowing what else to do, Matt repeatedly begged God not to allow it to happen. What Hunter prayed was love at the brink of crazy.

Seven days after the conversation with Matt, James and Hunter were driving down the road, and James apologized to his son for not being able to quit drinking. That's when Hunter revealed his radical prayer. "Dad, I have told God to take my life if that's what it takes for you to give yourself to Him."

James was devastated. The thought that his son would give up his life so he would come to know God was more than he could take. The Spirit of God grabbed James by the heart, and he broke down in tears like a child. "Hunter, you cannot do that!" James cried.

Hunter replied, "Dad, I already did."

Still crying and shaken by the emotional and spiritual earthquake he was experiencing, James told Charlene what their son offered to God when they returned home. Then he said, "I am not willing to be responsible for the world missing out on Hunter."

It was the last day James ever took a drink. The following morning he got up early, took the Bible off the shelf, and turned his life over to Christ. The help he had been reluctant to ask God for was no longer difficult to seek. Hunter called Matt three days later to say his father was a new man.

Today James has no fear of falling back into the old grind and now recognizes what's important. His future once bleak, James's is now filled with dreams. He gives no thought to his past failures as a husband and father. There is no need to ponder what is gone. Self-condemnation doesn't heal; God does. And James has been seeking Him for two years—sober.

Charlene is elated with her transformed husband. Broken hearts often translate into running feet. No one would have ever blamed Charlene for leaving; she had numerous reasons, all completely valid. Yet instead of regrets, this amazing woman has rewards for her faith in God and James. What once hurt her most was James's inability to live up to God's expectations of him as a husband and father. Not anymore. She always knew the day would come when James would be made new, even if she weren't alive to see it. That time is now, and their marriage is stronger than ever. True love won.

As for Hunter, he is attending a major college, where he mentors fellow students. He plans to attend seminary after graduation and loves Jesus more than ever before. I don't know whether God would have taken Hunter up on his offer. He sacrificed His own Son, Jesus, so we could have a relationship with Him. Yet I can't help but admire Hunter for being willing to literally put his life on the line to see someone else find salvation.

We hear stories about missionaries who gave up their lives to reach people in remote places overseas. But even in the West, where there are churches on almost every corner, we still need people like Hunter who love deeply enough to pray bold prayers and make sacrifices to see someone come to Christ.

Chapter 15

DEATH'S DOOR

MY GRANDFATHER USED to say, "Only the good die young." He had seen his share of death as a soldier overseas. His words and the stories he told of his fallen comrades always intrigued me. I didn't know why the good had to die at all, let alone young. My boyhood questions have followed me into adulthood. I know I am not the only one who wonders about death. Maybe it is not knowing how or when we will die that makes death a topic of such fascination and suspicion.

Some people consider the reality of death with clarity and fearlessness and live each day as though it will be their last (knowing one day it will be!). Others live in a state of denial, as though ignoring it will somehow prevent death from taking them by the hand. I believe this is where we are as a society. We have replaced the word *death* with more comfortable terms of endearment. We say people have passed away or departed.

Every year Americans spend billions of dollars on

lotions, potions, and exercise motions to make them-selves look younger and live longer. But no matter how hard we try to beat death, the fact remains that one day our hearts will quit beating.

The very young often don't think much about death because they feel a degree of invincibility. But as we get older, we realize more and more that death cannot be ignored. It is something we must make peace with. We see the reality of death on television almost daily: planes flying into skyscrapers, people jumping to their deaths, soldiers killed by roadside bombs, and attacks on peaceful protestors. We have seen bodies crushed by earthquakes and corpses littering city streets after disasters. Despite the evidence, or perhaps because of it, many people still manage to become desensitized to the fact that we all will die one day.

Some people believe death is the end of any and all existence, while others believe we simply exit this life and enter the next. No matter which side of the fence you're on, one thing is for certain: we all have an appoint-ment with death that cannot be canceled. Ready or not, it will certainly come.

I was in Atlanta a few years ago and went out to dinner with a large group. Sitting next to me was a doctor. Curious about his experiences with dying patients, I asked him what it was like to be with someone as he walked through death's door. As a Christian I always assumed people who were atheists or agnostics would turn to God if they had a last opportunity. This doctor, who was a Christian, said he often shared his faith with willing patients even though it is against protocol. Yet in his experience almost no one had embraced Christ in his final moments. "People who spend their lives resisting and rejecting God are like set concrete," he told me. "They most often die the same way they lived: in unbelief."

That night I lay in my hotel pondering his comment. I couldn't help but wonder what causes people to be so obstinate and how "set" I was myself. I had no idea at the time, but in less than six months I would know exactly what the good doctor meant.

Rick was a military man. He had spent several years in the air force and was now enjoying retirement. He was divorced, single, and alone except for the twenty-two-year-old son he allowed to live with him. Although he lived within blocks of my house, we were like strangers and knew only surface details about each other. We had casual, friendly conversation but never managed to talk about anything of substance. I was busy living my life while he casually lived his. One of the few things I knew for sure about Rick was that he was serious about exercise; every day he could be seen taking brisk walks through the neighborhood.

One spring morning, as I drove past him on my way to a meeting, I noticed a huge scar running down the back of his clean-shaven head. Later that day I saw another neighbor, and I inquired about what had happened to Rick. I found out he had been diagnosed with brain cancer and had recently undergone surgery. I was a little shocked at the report and felt guilty that I allowed someone in such close proximity to be so far away relationally.

I "accidentally" ran into Rick the next day and expressed my sympathy for the health challenges he was facing. I explained that I had just heard about his cancer diagnosis the previous day. He seemed optimistic about fighting the disease and remained hopeful about his future. As our visit winded down, I told him I would be praying for him. Although I was sincere, it felt like something was missing.

I wondered whether Rick believed in God and wanted to ask him the day we talked, but the timing felt wrong. I justified my procrastination by telling myself I would have the discussion in the next few weeks. My intentions were good, because I felt a responsibility to say something, but my actions, or lack thereof, were all wrong. I'm embarrassed to admit it, but several months passed by without me seeing Rick or stopping by to check on him. I did pray for him when he crossed my mind, but I was not diligent or consistent. I never eased his burdens by providing meals or doing anything else tangible. I was a really poor excuse for a neighbor.

As the summer started slowing down, my schedule began picking up. At one point I had been gone close to ten days straight and was chomping at the bit to return home to my family. When I arrived late that afternoon, cars were stacked up and down the street, and people were going in and out of Rick's home. I was getting my luggage out of the car when I saw Rick's son, Terry, walk out their front door.

I traipsed through his yard and stuck my foot in my mouth, as I jokingly asked if they were having a party. I felt like a complete idiot when he explained that his father had been given less than two weeks to live. How could I have been so thoughtless? How could I have not figured out what was going on? I told his son I wanted to see Rick and asked if I could come by. He said his dad was running low on energy, and he was just about to ask everyone to leave, but I would be welcome to visit the next day.

My family had not seen me in days. Normally when I am gone for an extended period of time, I take forty-eight hours and do nothing but hang out with Missy and the kids. But Rick couldn't wait. After giving everyone in my house a big hug, I asked them to come into the kitchen. I explained Rick's situation and told them I felt I had to see him immediately even though I had been asked to wait. There was no way I could live with my conscience if he died before morning. We all stood in the kitchen, held hands, and prayed for Rick to make peace with God if he hadn't already. As I hurried out of the house, I felt confident Rick would be receptive to what I was about to share.

When I knocked on the door, Terry looked surprised. Before he could speak, I apologized for not waiting until the next morning. I told him I needed to talk with Rick about urgent matters and asked if it would be all right. He asked me to wait at the door while he made sure his dad was up to the visit. When he returned, he said I was welcome, but I needed to make it short if possible. When I walked in, my nerves were jumping. In my entire life I have never had the opportunity to talk with someone who knew in advance he was days away from death.

I was surprised to find Rick sitting in the living room watching the game show *Wheel of Fortune*. It seemed a strange choice for someone with so little time left. As the host asked the contestants to spin the wheel, I asked Rick how he was feeling. He said he felt weak and sick but was keeping a positive attitude. He had lost a lot of weight, and the cancer's effects showed in his countenance as much as it did everywhere else. His eyes seemed faded, and the crow's feet around them seemed to leave a larger footprint than normal.

As I listened to his report from the doctors, I wondered how to communicate my thoughts. When he finished speaking, I hesitated, and an awkward silence hung in the room. Despite the huge lump in my throat and the dry sensation of cotton in my mouth, I tried to remain composed. But the harder I tried to hold back my emotion, the more difficult it became. Rick picked up on my struggle and briefly glanced away from the TV and directly at me.

Through a cracking voice and watery eyes I began to explain the reason for my visit. "I'm so sorry it has taken so long for me to stop by and even sorrier that we have never had what I believe to be the most important discussion in this life. I don't know what your thoughts are about God, faith, or eternal life, but I wanted to tell you what happened to me years ago that changed my life." I then gave a brief but thorough description of how I came to faith in Christ.

Rick never looked my direction the entire time I spoke, but when I finished talking, he turned his entire body toward me, moved his glasses to the top of his head, and looked directly in my eyes. "Jay, I appreciate you stopping by today. I know you are sincere and really care about what will happen to me after my death. I have seen you on television, and I respect you, your work, and your beliefs. You are very talented.

"However, I could never believe in Jesus Christ because of His statements about being the only way. It seems

186

unthinkable to me that there are billions of sincere people who could spend eternity in a place called hell because they were unwilling to believe in Jesus. I have my own beliefs about God, and since I do not believe there is any life after death, I guess it really doesn't make much difference what I think about Jesus." Rick wasn't being rude; he was just being honest. His weak, frail voice didn't hide the strength of his convictions.

I was breathing harder than usual from my surprise at his response. I even wondered for a moment if he was joking or testing me. Realizing he was serious, I leaned forward, put my elbows on my knees, and stammered out a plea. "Rick, I don't understand your rejection of God's gift. You are a privileged man to know the time line of your departure. Many will die in the next few weeks never having known death was coming, but you have a unique opportunity to be prepared and get your spiritual affairs in order. God wants a relationship with you and loves you deeply."

Rick smiled, rubbed his forehead with his fingers, and spoke gently. "Jay, I want to thank you again for stopping by, but I cannot believe as you do." I asked if I could pray for him, and he agreed. I did all I knew to do: I asked God to help Rick understand the path of salvation. We shook hands, and I thanked him for his willingness to listen. When I walked out the door, I immediately thought back to my conversation with the doctor in Atlanta.

Back at home I told my crew what Rick had said. Even the kids were confused. I didn't sleep much that night as I tried to process my conversation with Rick. No amount of reasoning enabled me to connect those disconnected wires, and Rick just continued to linger in my thoughts.

Two days later at 10:30 a.m. the doorbell rang. I looked through the front glass and saw Terry standing on the porch. As soon as I opened the door, Terry very stoically said, "I just wanted you to know we took Dad to the hospital last night because he wasn't doing well. About two hours ago he passed away." I offered my condolences and thanked him for letting me know. I promised to attend the memorial service and asked him to share the funeral details with me as soon as they were determined. Neither of us showed any emotion. After Terry left, I slid down the wall and began to cry. I couldn't stop wondering what Rick was experiencing as he began eternity.

Three days later I attended Rick's farewell service, which was held at a local funeral home. There were about thirty people there, with three of them sharing their memories of Rick. One was an old friend from the military who joked about the many times they drank too much. He said "wherever" Rick was, he was certain he was having a big party.

A woman told the audience to expect during difficult times for Rick to be like a little fairy on their shoulders who would offer words of encouragement. The man officiating said little to nothing about God until a final and brief prayer. Never before nor since that day have I attended a funeral where Scripture was not read. At the close of the service I walked past Rick's casket and silently said good-bye. As far as I knew, it would be the last time I would ever see him.

I am still jolted and frustrated by how quickly life can end. Three years after Rick's funeral I traveled to a rural part of Tennessee. After addressing several thousand teenagers over five days, I concluded the week with a talk at the local high school gymnasium we had rented. Churches sponsored the event, and we had standing room only despite the fact that three denominations boycotted my visit. I shared my personal story and concluded much the same way as I did with Rick, by offering people an opportunity to begin a relationship with Jesus. Close to three hundred people indicated their desire to know Christ personally.

Shortly after I arrived home, I received an urgent voice mail from a youth leader in the area. I called back immediately and could hear in his voice that he was shaken. He told me a terrible tragedy had occurred. A beautiful, curly-haired fourteen-year-old girl named Cathy went to a softball game with her cousin. By the game's end it had begun to rain, and they ended up driving home in a thunderstorm. Initially Cathy was in the front seat, but she moved to the back in order to make room for a guy who needed more legroom.

On their way home the car hit some standing water and hydroplaned off the road and straight into a tree. Cathy wasn't wearing a seat belt and was killed instantly. Her cousin, the driver, was severely injured, but no one else was killed. The youth leader told me that Cathy had attended our closing night event in the basketball arena and asked if I happened to meet her. When I told him we had never met, he shared the rest of the story.

Cathy heard me speak at her school and was considering going to our rally, but since she was overloaded with homework, she decided to stay at home. A friend called later and encouraged Cathy to go with her to the rally.

She agreed and was one of the hundreds who prayed that night to ask Jesus to invade their lives with His forgiveness and power. Cathy's mother, who has since become a friend of mine, said the night Cathy accepted Christ, she came home so excited. "Mom," she said, "we got to talk. Tonight I became a Christian, and I want to live the rest of my life for God. I want everything to be different!"

Those proved to be more than mere words. By everyone's account Cathy started attending a Bible study before school and was willing to tell anybody who would listen how God radically altered her life. At her funeral the entire account of her newfound faith was told, prompting many students to follow in her footsteps and surrender their lives to Christ. Her family gave me permission to tell her story during my talks, and numerous times I have put her picture on big screens where I was speaking. Because of Cathy's bold and unapologetic faith, multitudes have found life through her tragic death.

I am so glad Cathy didn't put off until tomorrow what she could do that day. It would have been so easy for her to choose to wait until she was older, possibly when she was in college or after she was married or when she felt more settled in life. It also would have been easier for Cathy to stay in the closet after committing her life to Jesus. She didn't have to be vocal and risk being ridiculed. But this lion-hearted teen wouldn't shrink back, even though she knew the brutal criticism teens are so prone to unleash on one another.

Thankfully Cathy's heart was not yet "set" in the concrete of unbelief. She still had the tenderness of spirit that too often evaporates the older people get. How different her experience must have been from Rick's when she looked into the face of God and heard Him say, "Well done, My good and faithful servant." Death does not end eternal relationships; it just alters them.

Just when I thought I was finished writing this chapter, I received a call. It had been only twenty-three hours since I wrote what I thought would be the last sentence when my cousin called to tell me his father had been given no more than four days to live. His father, Ronnie, is a great man with a huge, giving heart. He spent his life trying to help people in need; he's the type of guy who would literally give you the shirt off his back.

Ronnie had been tremendously successful in business and life. He was married to the same woman for decades and had two children who loved and respected him. He never had any serious health challenges and was unaware of any problem until three months ago when a doctor's visit revealed he had pancreatic cancer. He was willing to do whatever was necessary to fight the disease, and throughout his rounds of treatment he kept a positive outlook.

I ran into him at a sporting goods store just a few weeks before my cousin called, and you would never have known he was sick. His spirits were high, and he was feeling well enough to drive two hours to Dallas for a shooting competition. He told me optimistically that he was exploring every option, and because he was a fighter, he would never just give up and die. He believed he could win the war with cancer.

He remained energetic and active until the last week, when he started having trouble eating. Soon he was unable to keep food down. His doctor decided to feed him intravenously, but when they opened him up for the surgery, they found the cancer had spread so rapidly the procedure would be impossible. Unable to eat yet eaten up with cancer, Ronnie was given less than four days to live.

When my cousin called, I immediately made plans to visit Ronnie. As I drove to the hospice, I gave myself a pep talk about not getting emotional. I didn't want to add more sorrow to an already painful situation. Plus, Ronnie is a man's man who always manages his feelings and reactions well. I didn't want to embarrass myself.

When I walked in, Ronnie looked extremely thin, but there was an abiding peacefulness about him. His wife greeted me from one corner of the room and his son from the other. As I gave them both a hug, my mind started searching for words. I didn't want to say something hokey or insincere, but I wasn't sure what I should to a man who was standing at the edge of eternity. I made my way to the chair right next to Ronnie's bed.

Ronnie spoke first in his distinct baritone voice. "Thank you for coming, Jay. How are you doing, and how is that baby boy you were taking on a hunt?" I didn't reply. Despite the promises I made to myself, my attempts to remain emotionally strong were starting to unravel. I tried at least three times to keep my tears boxed up, but I couldn't even come close. After several intense seconds, I finally managed two meager words, "I'm sorry." He patted my hand and said, "Everything is fine. I know I am going to be with the Lord, and I'm ready."

I already knew he was a man who loved Jesus and would be welcomed by God in heaven, but even if I didn't know that I would have been convinced by the way Ronnie spoke and the look in his eyes. His son told me on the phone the previous night that Ronnie had been taking every opportunity to tell his friends about his faith in Christ. Ronnie continued patting the back of my hand until I could pull it together, and I knew he wasn't ashamed of my poorly controlled emotions.

Somehow through my breaking voice I managed to eke out a few words: "Ronnie, you are a good man. I have always respected you. I will never forget you calling me after I became a Christian. I had lost most of my old friends, and then you asked me to lunch. You encouraged me to stay the course, told me you were proud of me, and then gave me a gift to help get our organization started. I will always appreciate you, what you've done for me, and what you have stood for."

He nodded, and I could see a tear in his eyes. Several people were waiting for their turn to see him, and after getting a brief update on his prognosis, I knew I needed to go. "Ronnie, I will not tell you good-bye. I'm not good at saying them anyway. Good-byes are for people who will never see each other again, but I know for sure we will meet on the other side. So if it's OK with you, I'll just say, 'See you soon, my friend.'" He pulled me down and hugged me. I wiped the tears off my cheeks as I stood up and looked him in the eyes. Then we both just smiled.

When I reached my SUV, I began to think about the conversation I had with Rick on his deathbed. Ronnie and Rick died of the same disease but in completely different ways. I asked God to help me finish strong, like Ronnie did, and to leave a legacy of faith in my tracks. I wondered if God would give me the chance he gave Ronnie, to tell friends and family I loved them before taking my final breath. I wondered if I would leave a legacy.

More than ever I want to die with an echo. After my visit with Ronnie that day, I thought again that this life is nothing more than a dress rehearsal for the real thing and that I should always be ready. I've been shown my whole life how to live, but no one ever showed me how to die, until Ronnie.

Every time I get in front of an audience and look into the sea of faces, I always wonder how many are actually ready for the next life. Memories of past days and people still haunt me, like the older man in the Dallas-Fort Worth airport who had a stroke and fell dead on the concrete floor. Hearing the thud of his head hitting the floor made me sick to my stomach. I stood over his body until emergency personnel carried him away.

Or I think of the young man in his twenties who was thrown from his car while riding down a Louisiana highway. I watched him take his last breath as he lay on the scorching blacktop in a pool of blood. When the paramedics put a sheet over his body, I thought to myself that at that moment he was entering heaven or hell. I just stood there, unable to do anything but wonder.

The faces of death are so unforgettable, but then so are the faces of life. They give me an urgency I might otherwise never have known. Memories of the joyous grins and excited smiles on the faces of people who said yes to Christ are clearer than crystal. I remember the journey of the woman from Texas who found peace with God after becoming so desperate she tried to end her life by drinking radiator fluid. I still feel a rush of adrenaline when I think of eighteen-year-old Kyle. His father shot his mother in the head, giving vicious birth to Kyle's anger, drug addiction, and downward spiral toward prison. His turn to God was one of the most miraculous conversions I've ever witnessed.

And how could I ever forget Chase, from the small town of Borger, Texas? His parents invited him to come hear me speak, where he settled once and for all whether he would serve God. Seventy-two hours later he crashed his motorcycle into a car. He was flown by helicopter to Amarillo, where the doctors pronounced him brain dead and unable to exist on his own. That night he was taken off life support and ushered into the arms of Jesus. As he debated whether to surrender his life to Christ, he could never have known that in a matter of hours he would stand before God.

None of us existed forever in the past, but we will all exist forever in the future. Our eternity is not determined by what we do but by what we believe. What matters most is not if we are prepared for living, but if we are prepared for dying. It is not too late now, but someday it could be. My hope is that any uncertainty you may have about where you spend eternity will die a death of its own.

Chapter 16

TORNADO ALLEY

I GREW UP AND live in a region known as Tornado Alley. It's the expanse of land encompassing north Texas, Oklahoma, Kansas, and Nebraska, with my home state of Texas owning the regrettable reputation of having more twisters than any other. For outsiders the decision to live in this lion's den seems unreasonable, but for those of us who have sunk our roots here, it's a part of life.

Tornado watches and warnings are as common to us as spring bluebonnets, sultry red Indian paintbrushes, and the blooms of magnificent magnolia trees. The black and gray clouds that collide in the skies often provoke nothing more than aggravation that our favorite TV show is being interrupted by a weather forecaster. I don't like to admit it, but often when a tornado is reported to be on the ground, folks are more likely to go out in the front yard to get a good look than to take shelter in their bunker. I know these actions are worthy of criticism, but some dangers can become so commonplace they are no longer treated with the caution they deserve.

We do have contingency plans in place. During cyclone season children rehearse tornado drills at school, and the local news networks air severe weather specials so viewers will know the appropriate actions to take. Protocol is to move to the smallest room that is closest to the center of your home and cover up with pillows, blankets, and so on. We are told to never get near windows, mirrors, or exterior walls, and most of all, never try to outrun a tornado in your car. A vehicle is not adequate shelter, and, worse yet, you could inadvertently drive right into the lap of the storm.

I guess you shouldn't run from some trouble even when it's a tornado. The recommended response is to drop anchor and ride it out. On top of its other instructions, the city turns on its tornado alarms for testing on the first Monday of every month. It's an ear-pounding sound that temporarily drives most dogs to the edge of insanity. The shrill treble horns can torture their ears so much many begin howling like werewolves. More times than I care to admit, I have taken ornery pleasure in watching my Labrador retriever, with his chin pointed straight up to the sky and his mouth barely open, make long, wailing sounds.

Although "alley" veterans know a tornado can occur at any time, we can be like anyone else when it comes to tragedy. We wrongly assume that if something bad is going to happen, it won't happen to us. I think that's why some treat tornado watches like the boy who cried wolf. We've grown weary of false alarms. Like many other warnings in life, we see storms brewing in the distance with the potential to destroy, but we turn a deaf ear or blind eye.

The city of Wichita Falls, population 100,000, is stapled with oil wells, cattle, mesquite trees, horses, acres of golden wheat, an unimpressive chocolate waterfall, and at times dark, sinister clouds on the horizon. The weather code is increasingly difficult to decipher, especially during the warmth of springtime. I have spent most of my life living in its boundaries, except for short stints in Kansas City, Kansas, and San Antonio, Texas. It is a midsized town with a small-town feel. The Red River separates us from the Oklahomans who live twelve miles away, as does the deep-seated rivalry between the Sooners and Longhorns.

When you drive on the outskirts of Wichita, people in trucks will wave as if they know you. Respect for others is widespread, and decent men watch their language around women and children. At restaurants a stranger will often open the door for you. Southern hospitality is real here. Wichita doesn't possess the glamour or exhilaration of my two favorite cities, Los Angeles and New York, nor does it intoxicate my heart the way those cities do, but it's a decent, peaceful place to live. Everything is manageable, except for the oppressive summer heat...and the occasional death-hungry twister.

Neither my family nor anyone else in Wichita Falls could ever have fathomed the magnitude of storm headed toward our hometown on April 10, 1979. Though the day would become known as "Terrible Tuesday," it kicked off like any other. The warm Texas sun popped up like bread from a toaster; blue jays cawed, and long-tailed mockingbirds mimicked the songs of their cousins. Students went to class at Midwestern University, airmen from Sheppard

Air Force Base flew jets over the city, and baseball season was getting into full swing.

Later in the day the National Weather Service issued a familiar tornado watch at about the same time most bankers were returning to their offices from lunch. As for me, I attended school then was picked up by my mother and went home as always. Oblivious to any danger I watched television on the sofa until drifting off to a peaceful sleep.

At 5:45 p.m. the violent, percolating skies began to vomit golf-ball-size hail, which continued to spew for almost fifteen minutes. Many witnesses say the most eerie experience was the unnatural silence that settled across the town after the wind and hail completely died down around 6:00 p.m. A few ominous minutes later the tornado sirens were trumpeting their warning. The ambush from hell had been unleashed.

On the west side of the city three super-cell tornadoes merged to form one mammoth beast. This F-4 death monster conjured winds over 200 mph and measured more than a mile and a half wide as it began to kill hopes, dreams, and families: their past, present, and future. As the titan unleashed its initial fury across town, my mother got close to my face, grabbed me by both shoulders, shook me, and yelled, "Hurry, son, you've got to wake up."

Hearing the urgency in her voice, I asked, "What's going on?" Almost screaming, she said, "Don't ask questions; just go get in the car!" I wasn't completely awake as Mom and Dad frantically pushed my two sisters and me out the back door. When I stepped outside, I immediately noticed the sky looked smoky. Unaware of what was happening, I first thought the city was on fire. As we rushed to the car, I looked behind me and saw debris flying through the air. Then I knew.

As Dad slammed Mom's blue Lincoln Continental into reverse, both he and the tires began to screech. "Everybody get down, as low as you can." I heard his command, but it didn't stop me from rising up to look out the back window. I could feel pressure over my entire body similar to what your chest feels when you swim too deep.

Mom's car, which looked like a hearse, sounded like it was being hit by a jackhammer because of the missiles flying through the air. Dad pressed the gas pedal, but you could feel its horsepower being held back as the wind pushed against the car. It felt like someone tied a bungee cord to the rear bumper as the recoil surged us forward, backward, and side to side. At one point the car lifted off of the ground. The fear of death didn't just grab me; it enveloped me. Even though Dad reached into the backseat to push my head closer to the floorboard, I could still see objects ripping through the air around us. Power lines created a fireworks show as they snapped above us, and nearby roofs were popping off homes.

As Dad drove the car south, there was no way to be certain if we were headed into the mouth of the assassin or away from it. I continued to duck in the backseat until Dad began yelling about the people in front of us who were sitting at the red light waiting for it to change. Paralyzed by fear and conditioned by routine, they did nothing but wait and hope. Other well-intentioned people were turning on the street to go back in the direction we had just come from. It is likely that for many this decision was their last, since they were heading directly into the belly of the beast.

Unwilling to wait, Dad drove the Lincoln like it was an army tank and bolted right through the light, over the median, and into some oncoming traffic. For some unknown reason it made a strong impression on me when several cars honked at Dad as he raced to save his family. When we stopped in the middle of chaotic drivers, seconds grinded away like hours as Dad and Mom briefly debated whether to turn right or left.

Mom lobbied for the right while Dad argued to go left. Dad loved Mom, and she respected him and his decisions even when she didn't like them. He was never a dictator, and she wasn't anyone's doormat. They arrived at almost every decision mutually, but in the event they didn't agree, we all knew Mom would follow Dad's lead. Under the colossal, dirt-ridden skies Dad steered left, and Mom prayed aloud.

My racing heartbeat began to slow when I realized we were getting away from the storm. Speeding like a teenage boy who just got his driver's license, Dad hammered down the road until we reached the edge of the city and were out of harm's way. As it would happen, we ended up parking next to the Crestview cemetery. There we watched the death angel as it swept through town.

When the twister was no longer visible, we headed toward home. As we got close to our house, we began to wonder if it was still there. Mom kept telling Dad she knew it would be intact. When we were close enough to glimpse our neighborhood in the distance, Mom yelled dad's name. We all saw what the storm left in its wake. As calm as a summer night, Dad simply said, "Everything will be all right. Everything is OK."

My two sisters and I began to cry as stone cold reality

set in. Our four-bedroom house, our security, safe haven, and a portion of our childhood innocence had vanished. Just about everything except a couple of walls was sucked away. In the momentary confusion, my parents broke the rules. Trying to escape a tornado by car was opposite everything the experts recommended. Dad pointed toward a place that was formerly a room. It was where we were supposed to have taken shelter, proving that if we had stayed behind, none of us would have survived.

I knew there had been some divine intervention. The remains resembled a bomb site from a third world country. A city Dumpster sat in the middle of my room, and Mom's bright-red nightgown was blowing in one of the few remaining tree branches. Our two dogs were missing, along with most of our possessions. Almost everything had flown away or was repositioned, but some things were oddly still in place. Mom's Bible sat just where she had left it without a single page turned or missing.

The thing that tore Mom up more than anything was the disappearance of our childhood photos. She found a torn 8 x 10 picture of my baby sister and began to gently wipe it off as though the touch of her fingers would repair the damage. I can still see her crying as she looked down, tearfully telling my father, "They are irreplaceable."

My sisters and I stayed the night with my grandparents, Poppi and Mimi, in the tiny travel trailer where they lived. Although I slept with Poppi, I'd never felt more alone than I did that night. I didn't want to alarm my youngest sister, so I whispered when I asked my older sister if she thought the tornado was going to come back. Mom and

Dad slept in the back of Poppi's Ford truck because it had a camper and because there was no more room in the trailer. They seemed a million miles away.

The next morning Mom and Dad went with Poppi back to the site of our house to sift through the rubble and see what they could salvage. Mimi took us kids shopping for clothes because we had none except those on our backs. Most places were closed, but the TG&Y thrift store was open, and she purchased a few things to get us by. Mom always kept us dressed to the nines in name-brand clothes, but we appreciated anything we could get.

Later in the day someone from the *Fort Worth Star-Telegram* came to town to shoot some photos and caught my dad taking a breather from the cleanup. He was sitting in someone else's recliner that had flown into our yard and was still wearing the only clothes he had left, a suit and tie he wore to work the day before.

On the second day we lifted a mattress as part of the cleanup and found our dog Sugar trembling underneath. We walked past her for forty-eight hours, never knowing she was there because she never made a peep. She was traumatized until the day she died. From then on whenever rain fell or thunder sounded, we had to put her in a closet because she would become so erratic. Sugar wasn't alone. My youngest sister would also get a little tricky whenever the clouds began to churn.

When the carnage from the tornado was totaled, property damage mounted to $400 million. It traveled more than forty miles, stayed on the ground for more than an hour, and wiped out a fifth of the city before disintegrating in Oklahoma. In Wichita Falls alone, twenty thousand people were left homeless and forty-two were killed. The path it carved through town was more than two and a half miles long. The one it carved into our collective memory is without end.

One of the most disturbing things I learned about people came right after the storm. Law enforcement officials had to enforce a citywide curfew to stop people from looting. Mom and Dad parked Poppi's truck in the driveway and slept in the back so Dad could fend off thieves. It was inconceivable to me, a young sheltered boy who believed everyone was basically good, that people would take advantage of those who were most vulnerable.

Several days later, around the time we had finished rescuing whatever was worth keeping, Dad found a room for us at a local hotel. We lived there as refugees for two months before moving into another one for an additional month. Eventually we found a new house and turned it into a new home.

"Terrible Tuesday" is not just a page in the past, as people often describe tragedy. It is so much more. It's a part of my life that will never be forgotten, and it has shaped my perspective of the future. On April 10, 1979, my father came to a crossroads where he was forced to make a decision. This decision would determine his fate and that of his family. He didn't know it at the time, but everything was at stake.

In a similar way everyone faces a crossroads that requires him to make a choice that will impact him for eternity. We all come to this place, a point at which we must decide whether to receive Christ as our Savior. Only you can make that choice. Only you can choose to commit your life to Him. Your religious background, church, and parents cannot believe for you.

Some people dismiss their rejection of Christ, saying they want to wait until they are ready to truly submit to Him. But this is nothing more than a procrastination attempt.

Maybe you're reluctant to put your faith in Christ because of past hurts inflicted by people who called themselves Christians, or maybe a church hurt you. The pain you feel may be justified, but rejecting Jesus never is. Unlike those who love you as long as you love them, Jesus offers us love that is unconditional.

If you persist in despising Him, He still will love you! He proved it when He willingly laid down His life to pay for your mistakes. Two thousand years ago He suffered a brutal death because we needed something we could never obtain on our own: forgiveness.

When Roman soldiers nailed Jesus to a cross, everyone turned away from Him, including His Father. Jesus died and stayed in the grave until His Father brought Him back to life three days later. He is alive now and waiting for you to turn to Him by faith. It's more than praying a prayer and being baptized, sprinkled, or confirmed. It is complete surrender of your life to do His will and purposes. Yes, it would require you to give up anything standing in the way, but it would enable you to receive all that He is.

Could this book have landed in your hands so you could realize Christ is the answer you have been searching for? Perhaps at this very moment your heart is yearning for His peace and forgiveness. If so, and if you are willing to let go of your sin, He will give you the peace you seek. I encourage you right now to ask Jesus to forgive you. Tell Him in your own words that you believe He died for you,

He is alive, and He is God's Son. Invite Jesus to come into your life.

Don't worry about saying a perfect prayer; just be real and honest. Maybe you think it's too late or that Jesus would be unwilling to accept you, but He made a promise that you can take to the bank: "Anyone who comes to Me, I will never cast away." (See John 6:37.) I hope you won't put your relationship with God off until "tomorrow." Tomorrow may never come.

Perhaps you put faith in Christ years ago but took a wrong turn somewhere along the way. Maybe at one time your relationship with God was strong, sincere, and exciting, but that was a long time ago. The things you thought would bring happiness have only left you feeling more incomplete than before. At night or when you're alone, you sometimes wonder if God could ever restore and release you from the hurts, pains, addictions, discouragement, anger, bitterness, and guilt that crush your hope. God does not resent you. He doesn't hate you, and more than anything else He wants you to come home.

In Luke 15 a story is told about a wasteful, disobedient son who ran away from his dad. In the story the father doesn't condemn the runaway son upon his return but wraps him in welcoming arms. He doesn't give him a lecture or put him on a guilt trip but holds a celebration for him instead. Your Father is just like this. He is eagerly waiting for you to come home.

Maybe you lost the map and don't know how to start the journey back toward Christ. Your starting place is asking God to forgive you and enable you to turn away from the things keeping you adrift. Ask Him to show you the specific sins separating you from Him and confess them. He promises to forgive every wrong you have committed.

I have realized through the years that, just like the looters after the tornadoes, there is a thief on the prowl that wants to steal, annihilate, and murder our present, past, and future. And he targets people during times of trouble to take advantage of them. If you do not stay on guard as my dad did, this spiritual enemy will crush you.

For years I allowed this crook named Satan to rob me of the life God intended for me. I now know I didn't have to permit him to steal from me, and neither do you. This murderer is deceptive and very conniving. He is a master at blinding people's minds from the truth about God's Son. He is working overtime to prevent you from experiencing God's love and forgiveness.

Only God's truth can free people from these lies. The warning has sounded, and the escape route has been laid out. What you or I do about it is up to us. I pray you make the right decision at this intersection. Turn away from the storm and rush toward the path of salvation.

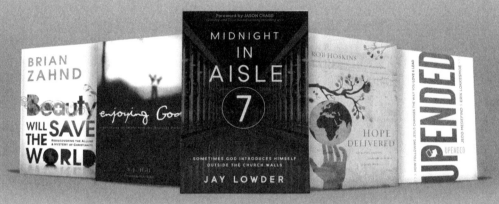